MW00995517

Enjoy this little slice of Baltimore

Best Wishes for an outstanding 2015!

Yvonne and team

EXTRAORDINARY RECIPES FROM

BALTIMORE CHEF'S TABLE

KATHY WIELECH PATTERSON & NEAL PATTERSON

Photography by Kevin Maher

CHARM CITY AND THE SURROUNDING COUNTIES

LYONS PRESS
Guilford, Connecticut
An imprint of Globe Pequot Press

Copyright © 2014 Morris Book Publishing, LLC

Lyons Press is an imprint of Globe Pequot Press.

All photography by Kevin Maher, Seven Set Studios,
except those on pages i, ii-iii, xi, xv, xvi, 168, 179, and
208, licensed by Shutterstock.com

Editor: Tracee Williams
Project Editors: Lynn Zelem and Lauren Brancato
Text Design: Libby Kingsbury
Layout Artist: Nancy Freeborn

Library of Congress Cataloging-in-Publication Data is
available on file.

ISBN 978-0-7627-9224-5

Printed in the United States of America
10 9 8 7 6 5 4 3 2 1

Restaurants and chefs often come and go, and
menus are ever changing. We recommend you call
ahead to obtain current information before visiting
any of the establishments in this book.

To Milo and Julie

Contents

Recipes by Course

Introduction

Not so long ago, it seemed that dining out in Baltimore involved one of three things: crabs, Continental cuisine, and fast food. There weren't many other choices, except for the rare jaunt to Chinatown (when Baltimore still had a Chinatown) for moo goo gai pan or some other gloppy Americanized dish, or to Little Italy for a plate of ravioli or a hefty portion of lasagna.

With the city perched on top of the Chesapeake Bay, blue crabs reigned supreme in Baltimore and were best devoured at brown-paper- or newspaper-covered tables in local crab joints like Connolly's, Bud's, or Obrycki's. The crabs were served piping hot and covered in mounds of spice and salt. Heaven forbid you cut your fingers on the shells, or your hands would burn for the rest of the night. And the spice created a tingle on the lips that made you grab for an ice-cold beer, preferably the then-locally-produced National Bohemian, affectionately known to one and all as Natty Boh. Connolly's, a crab shack along Pratt Street on Pier 5 in Baltimore's Inner Harbor, was one of the favorite dining spots of Baltimore's beloved mayor William Donald Schaefer. In fact, he ate there every week with his mother until she passed away. Connolly's met its own demise in 1991, with the building razed to make way for the Columbus Center.

During Bud's heyday, people waited in line for hours to eat the steamed crabs at Highlandtown native and World War II veteran Bud Paolino's eponymous restaurant, which faded away in the '90s. And Obrycki's, long synonymous with steamed crabs to generations of Baltimore visitors, closed its original seasonally-open Pratt Street location in 2011 and now offers crab cakes and crab balls at BWI Thurgood Marshall Airport and Cleveland Hopkins International Airport, of all places.

Then there was "Continental cuisine," a general term given to an amalgamation of the cuisines of Western Europe served at most of Baltimore's finer dining establishments during the twentieth century. The menu at Miller Brothers, which opened in 1913, offered such delights as chicken a la king, vichyssoise, and sauerbraten with red cabbage and boiled noodles. Known as "the place to eat," the restaurant also served exotic meats like squab, black bear, and pheasant. After fifty years, Miller Brothers closed in 1963.

Haussner's, another extremely popular restaurant of the time, had a successful seventy-three-year run. Even today, some fifteen years after the restaurant closed its doors for the last time, people still reminisce fondly about that delectable strawberry pie, topped with a wreath of whipped cream and garnished with toasted almonds. Also memorable was William Henry and Frances Wilke Haussner's collection of art, which decorated the restaurant's walls and included important works by European and American masters. This made a meal at Haussner's much like attending a fancy dinner party in the middle of an art gallery. The menu, too, was a work of art, boasting more than four hundred dishes including German-inflected schnitzels and sauerbraten and such exotica as pig's knuckles, frog's legs, and sweetbreads. Entrees came with one or two vegetables of the diner's choice from a list that included sauerkraut, stewed tomatoes, and fried eggplant. And then there was that giant ball of string pieced together by Haussner's employees from three-hundred-some miles of leftover twine. Haussner's closed in 1999, and the art collection—including the ball of string—was auctioned off by Sotheby's.

Nobody can accuse Baltimore of not being quirky.

Maison Marconi, a favorite dining spot of the opinionated Baltimore-born American journalist H.L. Mencken, was another bastion of Continental cuisine. Their menu had a bit of an Italian bent, gilded with luxurious dishes like the famous Lobster Cardinale, which involved chunks of lobster bathed in a rich sauce of egg yolks, heavy cream, and sherry and served in their own shells. For dessert one could have the best hot fudge sundae in town, swathed in luscious dark chocolate. Baltimore Orioles owner Peter Angelos bought the restaurant in 2000, promising to move the eighty-year-old landmark to a new location. That never happened, and as with all of the other long-gone restaurants, all we have left are memories.

The fast-food portion of the program, reserved for when Mom didn't feel like cooking, involved all of the usual suspects around today, but also included pizzerias and steakhouse chains like Sizzler and Ponderosa. For some reason our parents thought these joints were a swell place to have dinner at least once every couple of weeks; this engendered a real dislike for steaks and salad bars in our young minds that persists to this day.

That steakhouse wariness is about the only thing the two of us had in common, culinarily speaking, as we were growing up. Neal, who spent his formative years in Dundalk, in Baltimore County, was subjected to enough cheap steak that he thought perhaps he didn't really like food all that much if that was all there was to it. Conversely, Kathy, a city girl from Fells Point, grew up with a father who was eager to explore foreign cuisines other than Italian and German. While her parents liked cheap steak, too, more often they dined at places like Szechuan, which opened in the early '80s and may have been the first Baltimore restaurant serving something even resembling the cuisine of China's Sichuan Province, or Nichi Bei Kai, a local Japanese teppanyaki chain where the shrimp-flipping chefs thrilled Kathy and her younger brother, David. Spicy chicken and soy-flavored bean sprouts were welcome arrivals on a palate that was already used to eating her grandmother's Polish cooking and foods that wouldn't be considered particularly kid-friendly now, like bone marrow and beets.

After meeting in 1998, Kathy introduced Neal to Indian food and sushi, which opened his eyes (and stomach) to a whole new world of flavors. And that's pretty much what's been happening with the Baltimore dining scene since then. Continental cuisine, with its meat-and-two-veg approach to fine dining, is a thing of the past, and restaurants are embracing a different perspective on food. The juxtaposition of classic French and Italian technique with locally sourced ingredients and pinches of global or regional seasonings has popularly become known as New American or Modern American cuisine. It takes the dishes of the melting pot—pasta, tacos, stir-fries, stews—and combines them to form a uniquely American flavor profile.

You'll find, in the pages of this book, restaurants of all persuasions. There are those that serve Modern American cuisine and those that serve more straightforward comfort food. (Some will argue that putting lobster or truffles on mac and cheese makes the

dish both things.) There are also restaurants that serve food of a particular nation, like Italy or Cuba or Japan, and still others that celebrate the cooking of a particular region of the United States. Some are fancy and some are more casual. There's even a couple of bakeries and a food truck. None of them could be considered Continental restaurants, nor crab houses, nor fast food. All of them are an integral part of the Baltimore restaurant scene today.

BALTIMORE CITY

ALDO'S RISTORANTE ITALIANO

306 S HIGH STREET
BALTIMORE, MD 21202
(410) 727-0700
ALDOSITALY.COM
OWNERS: THE VITALE FAMILY
CHEF: SERGIO VITALE

Many Baltimoreans, when thinking about Little Italy, conjure up images of the generations-old classic red-sauce joints that dot High Street. These folks obviously haven't been to Aldo's, a relative newcomer to the neighborhood. Fifteen years ago,

when the restaurant opened, it was upscale when Baltimore didn't have very many places serving foie gras and truffles in an elegant Rita St. Clair–designed interior. Everyone said Aldo's would fail, and indeed the Vitales weren't exactly raking it in during the early months. But they persevered, concentrating on the elegant preparations that have since put them on the map.

Aldo's isn't the Vitale family's first restaurant. Patriarch Aldo Vitale owned a restaurant in Baltimore County and then ran a wholesale bakery that supplied pastries to places like Nordstrom Cafe and Dean & Deluca. Eventually the family found a pair of abandoned properties in Little Italy that seemed like the ideal location for a new restaurant. Aldo's Ristorante Italiano opened after nearly a year of renovation, including beautiful woodwork and a mahogany bar crafted by Aldo himself.

Sergio Vitale, Aldo's son, now runs the kitchen, after quietly "firing" his father a few years ago. It seems that everyone in town knows Sergio, a friendly bear of a man who knows food, appreciates food, and loves to talk about it. At lunch one afternoon we chatted about the local dining scene and where his restaurant fits in. There was some discussion about the recent surge in farm-to-table dining, to which Sergio remarked, "We just call it Italian food." Indeed, Aldo's has worked with local farmers and purveyors since the beginning; the restaurant also cures its own sopressata and pancetta as well as making most of its pasta in-house.

Sergio's approach to Italian food is pretty classic, yet modernized. Aldo's best-selling dishes are the eggplant tower—an elegant reinterpretation of eggplant Parmesan—a silky pappardelle in a rich wild boar ragù, and veal Milanese made from a giant veal chop. "I like to take something simple and expected and make it unexpected. Reimagined, but not nouvelle or molecular. We're not out to reinvent the wheel."

Orecchiette with Broccoli Rabe & Mild Italian Sausage

(SERVES 4)

One of the best-selling dishes at Aldo's, the orecchiette is also the recipe most requested by employees.

1 pound broccoli rabe, florets and tender stems only (discard fibrous stem ends)
2–3 links mild Italian sausage
¼ cup plus 2 tablespoons extra virgin olive oil (divided)
6 large garlic cloves, crushed and minced very finely (divided)
1 cup chicken stock
1 pound orecchiette pasta
¼ teaspoon crushed red pepper flakes
¼ teaspoon salt
½ cup freshly grated pecorino Romano cheese

Blanch the broccoli rabe in boiling salted water for 20–30 seconds. Remove broccoli and plunge it into an ice water bath to cool it instantly. When cool, remove the broccoli rabe from the water, wrap it in a cloth towel, and wring out all excess moisture until dry. Cut broccoli rabe into ½-inch pieces and reserve.

Remove the sausage meat from its casings; discard the casings. Heat 2 tablespoons of the extra virgin olive oil in a medium-sized nonstick sauté pan over medium-high heat. When the oil is hot, add one-quarter of the minced garlic and the sausage meat. Using a wooden spoon or potato masher, crumble the sausage meat as it cooks so that it separates into individual cooked pieces as opposed to a solid mass. Cook 7–12 minutes or until browned and cooked through; remove from heat and reserve.

Heat the chicken stock to a simmer.

Cook the orecchiette in a large pot of boiling salted water until al dente (10–12 minutes); drain well, but reserve 2–4 tablespoons of the cooking liquid.

As the orecchiette cooks, heat the remaining ¼ cup of olive oil over high heat in a large, deep sauté pan. Add the remaining minced garlic and cook until golden. As soon as the garlic becomes golden, immediately add the reserved broccoli rabe, sausage, red pepper, and hot chicken stock. Cook for 4–6 minutes, stirring occasionally. Salt to taste.

Add the cooked orecchiette to the skillet along with 1–2 tablespoons of the pasta cooking liquid and toss over medium-high heat for 1–3 minutes, stirring constantly. Remove from heat and toss with grated pecorino cheese, stirring constantly, until the cheese melts and becomes incorporated into the "sauce." Serve immediately. Top with more grated pecorino cheese to taste.

Alewife

21 N Eutaw Street
Baltimore, MD 21201
(410) 545-5112
ALEWIFEBALTIMORE.COM
OWNERS: Daniel Lanigan, Bryan Palombo
CHEF: Chad Wells

The west side of Baltimore's downtown got a much needed lift when the Hippodrome, an old movie palace, was remodeled into a beautiful venue for Broadway shows and other events. The area later became a mini theater district when the Everyman Theatre moved in around the corner. All that was needed was a comfortable restaurant and watering hole for theater patrons and local office workers alike to hang out at suppertime. Enter Alewife.

Situated in an old bank building, the high ceilings, hardwood floors, and polished wood bar and counters put you in mind of an age when the Hippodrome may have hosted the best vaudeville acts. Of course, we don't think patrons of that era would be familiar with the forty-plus beers on Alewife's menu. Nor would they expect dinner offerings like the top-selling Smoke Burger: eleven ounces of locally raised beef, smoked Gouda and gruyère, bacon, caramelized onions, and chipotle aioli on a brioche bun. The sandwich is so popular, Chef Chad Wells says the restaurant goes through 2,000 pounds of ground beef per month.

While beef is a big seller, so is fish. Chef Wells, an Ellicott City native, is passionate about the environment. He's also passionate about fishing and has even appeared on the Cooking Channel's *Hook, Line & Dinner.* So when the local waters became infested with snakeheads, a highly destructive invasive species from Asia that can survive and even walk on land, he felt that a good way to beat them would be . . . to eat them. The same goes for blue catfish. If overfishing can destroy other fish populations, why not these two species that don't belong in our waters? Luckily,

the idea caught on. "Snakehead is a great seller," says Chef Wells. "I can't keep it in stock." In fact, people so loved the idea of dining on these frankenfish, Alewife had to sell tickets to its inaugural snakehead dinner via a lottery.

"I'm a fisherman. I love to do it. And if I can use it to benefit everyone around us, it's awesome."

FRANKENFISH TACOS
WITH BLISTERED CORN SALSA, CHIPOTLE SLAW
& CRISPY SWEET POTATO STRINGS

(MAKES 6 TACOS, SERVES 2–3)

At Alewife, Chef Wells uses invasive species like snakehead or blue catfish in these tacos, but you can use any Maryland fish.

For the fish and chimichurri marinade:

¼ cup white vinegar
2 teaspoons dried oregano
½ tablespoon crushed red pepper
½ tablespoon kosher salt
7 cloves garlic, peeled
1½ bunches fresh flat-leaf parsley, stemmed
Juice of 1 lime
¾ cup extra virgin olive oil
1 (12-ounce) skinless snakehead fillet,
    sliced into 1-inch-thick slices

For the blistered corn salsa:

1 medium onion, cut in small dice
2 ears Maryland corn, grilled until blistered,
    kernels removed
Juice of 2 limes
8 ripe tomatoes, seeded and diced
1 jalapeño, seeded and finely diced
¼ bunch fresh cilantro, stemmed and
    roughly chopped
Kosher salt

For the slaw:

1½ cups mayonnaise
2 tablespoons granulated sugar
2 tablespoons white vinegar
1½ tablespoons pureed chipotle in adobo
½ tablespoon fresh lime juice
½ head cabbage, shaved

For the sweet potato strings:

1 sweet potato
Oil for deep frying

For assembly:

6 (6-inch) corn tortillas
Canola oil, for cooking fish
Kosher salt
Fried sweet potato sticks
Lime wedges

To marinate the fish: Combine the vinegar, oregano, crushed red pepper, salt, garlic, parsley, and lime juice in a food processor. Slowly add in the olive oil while blending.

Cover the snakehead with half of the chimichurri marinade and refrigerate while preparing the corn salsa and slaw. (Refrigerate remaining marinade up to 3 days for another use.)

To make the salsa: Combine the onions, corn, lime juice, diced tomato, jalapeño, and cilantro in a mixing bowl and season with salt. Taste and adjust the seasoning as necessary.

To make the slaw: Whisk together the mayonnaise, sugar, vinegar, chipotle, and lime juice in a bowl until combined. Slowly add the sauce mix to the shaved cabbage until the desired consistency is reached. If you would like more heat, add more chipotle puree.

To make the sweet potato strings: Peel sweet potato. Using a mandoline, cut the potato into thin julienne strips. Alternately, if you have mad knife skills, you can cut thin slices from the potato, and then cut those slices crosswise into thin strips.

Heat oil to 350°F. Add potato strips in batches and fry until crispy. Remove potatoes from oil and drain on paper towels.

To cook the fish and assemble: Grill the tortillas on an outdoor grill or hot grill pan, or toast over an open flame until pliable and, if not using immediately, keep warm.

Heat a sauté pan over high heat and coat with oil. Once the pan is hot and the oil slides freely across the pan, place the snakehead slices in the pan and sprinkle with salt. Cook until the fish is tender to the touch and begins to flake when pushed with a spatula. This fish cooks extremely fast!

Place the grilled tortillas on a plate and top with the snakehead, salsa, slaw, and sweet potato strings. Serve with lime wedges.

Feral Hog Banh Mi Sliders

(MAKES 16 SLIDERS)

While the restaurant uses feral hog or wild boar for these sliders, you could use another meat, like turkey or pork. You could also make larger burgers with this recipe, but don't make patties over 6 ounces or so, because the very lean meat could dry out very quickly over high heat.

For the ginger dressing (makes about 4 cups):

½ cup Dijon mustard
½ cup low-sodium soy sauce
1 cup white vinegar
¾ cup brown sugar
2 tablespoons grated fresh ginger, preferably grated
    with a Microplane to equal 2 tablespoons
1 cup olive oil
¼ cup Asian toasted sesame oil

For the pickled carrot salad:

1 cup white vinegar
1 cup granulated sugar
1 teaspoon red pepper flakes
1 pound carrots, shaved or sliced very thinly
1 bulb fennel, shaved or sliced very thinly
Handful of daikon sprouts or radish sprouts
    (found in Asian groceries)
Handful of fresh cilantro leaves
Ginger dressing, to coat

For the burgers:

1 ounce fresh ginger, cut into small chunks
3 cloves garlic, peeled
2½ tablespoons sesame oil
2 tablespoons chopped chives
2 tablespoons kosher salt
2½ pounds ground feral hog or wild boar
16 brioche slider buns or dinner rolls

To make the ginger dressing: Place the mustard, soy sauce, vinegar, brown sugar, and ginger in a blender and puree until smooth.

Slowly add the olive oil to the mixture while the blender is running. Once all of the olive oil is incorporated, slowly add the sesame oil while blender is running.

Note: This dressing is also great for other salads, and as a glaze for grilled meats.

To make the pickled carrot salad: Combine the vinegar and sugar in a saucepan and boil until the sugar has dissolved. Stir in the red pepper flakes.

Put the carrots in a large bowl and pour the vinegar mixture over. Refrigerate until ready to use.

Note: These carrots last for a long time in the refrigerator. For long-term storage, pour the carrots and vinegar mixture into a wide-mouth jar with a lid.

Once the carrots are cold, drain and mix them in equal quantity with the shaved fennel. Toss with the sprouts, cilantro, and enough of the ginger dressing to coat everything lightly.

To make the burgers: In a blender or food processor, blend the ginger, garlic, sesame oil, chives, and salt until smooth.

Mix the ground boar with the ginger-garlic mixture until thoroughly combined. Form the meat into 2½-ounce patties and grill to desired doneness. Serve on toasted brioche buns topped with pickled carrot salad.

ALEXANDER'S TAVERN

710 S BROADWAY
BALTIMORE, MD 21231
(410) 522-0000
ALEXANDERSTAVERN.COM
OWNER: CHARLIE GJERDE
CHEF: FAITH PAULICK

The Gjerde brothers, Charlie and Spike, opened and closed several popular restaurants over the past two decades. Among them were Spike & Charlie's, jr., Atlantic, Joy America Cafe, and Hudson Street Baking Company. Today the two are still in the restaurant business, but they own separate restaurants in different parts of Baltimore City. Charlie's got Fells Point covered with his bar-restaurant, Alexander's Tavern.

Situated in two converted rowhouses in the shade of the Broadway Market, Alexander's combines the good-natured coziness of a typical narrow Fells Point bar with casual family dining in a separate room next door. Upstairs there's another bar, with a game room that includes shuffleboard and darts and that doubles as their private party room.

Chef Faith Paulick, a native Marylander from Harford County, developed her passion for food while working in restaurants to pay for her college education. Originally hoping to be a teacher, Faith instead moved to North Carolina to learn about upscale home-style cooking. But her biggest culinary inspiration comes from her grandmothers. Her maternal grandmother, a woman with a "sassy brash cast-iron-pan-waving attitude" taught her to take plain ingredients and turn them into something special with a little ingenuity and lots of love. Her paternal grandmother specialized in Pennsylvania Dutch baking techniques and instilled in Faith both the organization and the precision that are invaluable to a professional chef.

With this priceless training, Chef Paulick creates weekly specials like personalized peach pies and Maryland BLT sandwiches with Eastern Shore soft-shell crabs and local fried green tomatoes. But Alexander's Tavern is probably best known for its potato tots. More than one million of the crusty potato bites have been sold, most of them smothered in crab dip and melted cheese. A bit of Maryland tradition mingling with a childhood favorite.

MARYLAND TOTS

(SERVES 2)

Alexander's Tavern is famous for its potato tots, and this version, smothered in Baltimore crab dip and melted cheese, is the number one favorite.

4 ounces cream cheese

1 ounce heavy cream

1 tablespoon Old Bay seasoning, or to taste

1 teaspoon Worcestershire sauce

1 teaspoon sherry

1 teaspoon lemon juice

1 teaspoon crab base

6 ounces potato tots

Oil for deep-frying

Salt, to taste

2 ounces jumbo lump crabmeat

2 ounces cheddar jack cheese

In a saucepan over low heat combine the cream cheese, heavy cream, Old Bay, Worcestershire sauce, sherry, lemon juice, and crab base until melted and combined.

Deep-fry the potato tots until golden brown. Drain on paper towels and salt to taste. Place the tots in an ovenproof bowl or pie plate and smother with the crab dip mixture. Top with the lump crab and cheese.

Broil until the cheese is golden brown and bubbly.

ATWATER'S

529 E BELVEDERE AVENUE
BALTIMORE, MD 21212
(410) 323-2396
ATWATERS.BIZ
OWNER: NED ATWATER
HEAD BAKER: DYLAN MEYERS
HEAD PASTRY CHEF: JESS PLACEK
PLOUGHBOY KITCHEN HEAD: CHEF DAVID BEARD

Belvedere Square was a popular shopping destination in the '90s, but rising rents eventually sent merchants looking for more affordable venues. The Market became a ghost town. Fortunately for north Baltimore City, the shopping center changed hands and reopened in 2003, with Ned Atwater's bakery as one of the new tenants. "I have always wanted to be a part of the city market system. We were planning to move away from our wholesale location and looked at another of the city markets that was full at the time. Belvedere Square Market was vacant, having been closed for about ten years. This gave us the added opportunity to be part of building a food center for the community from scratch.

"We went into Belvedere baking bread and pastries and making a few pots of soup a day," Atwater says. "Soon customers asked for salads, then sandwiches, cheese, coffee and tea, and it just grew from there. More neighborhoods wanted good healthy food. So far it's working." We'll say. The business exploded from 6 employees in 2003 to 145 in 2013, including soup chefs and sandwich makers along with the bakery staff, all of whom are involved in testing and perfecting recipes. Besides Belvedere Square, there are now Atwater's shops in Kenilworth, Catonsville, and two locations on Falls Road in Bare Hills, just north of the city line. And let's not forget the various farmers' markets that Atwater's participates in each week.

Atwater, who has cooked for presidents Bill Clinton and George H. W. Bush, picked up a respect for buying local when he worked under Chef Michel Beaupin at King's Contrivance. "We support the community of farmers and producers that we have come to know at the farmers' markets that we participate in." A list of those sources, including Cherry Glen Farm, Walton's Seafood, Springfield Farm, and Black Rock Orchard, can be found on the company's website. These fresh ingredients, coupled with great service, are what keeps customers flocking to Atwater's. Personally, we like the fact that we know where everything comes from, even the nonlocal ingredients. And we love that Atwater's provides one-stop shopping for a fantastic, easy dinner: a couple quarts of soup, a cheese or two, a loaf of their delicious struan (a hearty, slightly sweet multigrain bread), and a fruit tart or cake for dessert.

BROWN SUGAR SPICED CAKE WITH BROWN BUTTER CREAM CHEESE ICING & BUTTERSCOTCH SAUCE

(SERVES 8–10)

To make this cake look as professional as possible, it helps to have several 8-inch cardboard cake rounds on hand as well as a cake turntable to make icing an easier task.

For the cake:

3 sticks (¾ pound) unsalted butter, at room temperature
2½ cups light brown sugar
1½ teaspoons cinnamon
½ teaspoon nutmeg
1½ teaspoons salt
1 tablespoon vanilla extract
4 large eggs
2¼ cups all-purpose flour
1½ cups cake flour
1¼ teaspoons baking powder
¾ teaspoon baking soda
1¼ cups buttermilk
½ tablespoon dark unspiced rum

For the icing:

3 sticks (¾ pound) unsalted butter, at room temperature (divided)
2 cups light brown sugar
½ teaspoon salt
1 cup heavy cream
½ cup powdered sugar
2 teaspoons vanilla extract
1¼ pounds cream cheese

For the butterscotch sauce:

¾ cups light brown sugar
½ cup corn syrup
¼ teaspoon salt
5 tablespoons unsalted butter
½ cup heavy cream
2 tablespoons dark unspiced rum

For assembly:

2–3 cups toasted chopped pecans

To make the cake: Preheat oven to 350°F. Butter and flour two 8-inch round cake pans.

In a large bowl or in the bowl of a stand mixer, cream together the butter, brown sugar, cinnamon, nutmeg, salt, and vanilla until fluffy. Add the eggs one at a time until each is fully incorporated.

In another bowl, sift together the flours, baking powder, and baking soda.

In a third bowl, combine the buttermilk and rum.

Alternately add the dry ingredients and buttermilk to the butter-sugar mixture in stages: dry, wet, dry, wet, finishing with dry.

Divide the batter evenly between the cake pans. Bake for 30–38 minutes, until a toothpick inserted in the center of the cakes comes out clean. Allow to cool in the pans for 5 minutes before turning them out onto racks to cool completely.

To make the icing: Place 2 sticks of butter in a saucepan and cook over medium-low heat until browned and nutty smelling. Add the sugar and salt and bring to a boil. Add the cream, reduce the heat, and simmer for 5 minutes, stirring constantly. Pour into a shallow pan and refrigerate until cool.

Cream together the remaining stick of butter, the powdered sugar, and the vanilla until light and fluffy.

Add the cream cheese and beat on medium until lump free. Add the cooled brown butter mixture and beat on medium-low speed until combined.

To make the butterscotch sauce: Combine the sugar, corn syrup, salt, and butter in a saucepan. Bring to a boil. Stir to ensure that all the sugar is melted. Add the cream and rum. Return to a boil and allow to boil for 5 minutes.

To assemble the cake: Slice the tops off both cake layers to create flat surfaces. Cut each layer in half horizontally to form four cake layers total.

While the butterscotch sauce is still warm, spread approximately ¼ cup on one side of each layer. Do not stack, but refrigerate the layers until the sauce is set. This will prevent the layers from sliding during icing.

Assemble the cake by placing one layer, sauce side up, on a plate (or cake turntable, if you have one). Spread ½ cup of icing on the sauced side. Top with another layer and another ½ cup of icing. Continue until all layers are stacked. Top with additional icing and spread more lightly on the sides. Grab handfuls of pecans and press them into the icing on the sides of the cake for garnish.

BIRROTECA

1520 CLIPPER ROAD
BALTIMORE, MD 21211
(443) 708-1934
BMOREBIRROTECA.COM
OWNER: CHEF ROBBIN HAAS

The quiet neighborhood of Woodberry, in northern Baltimore City, is fast becoming a restaurant destination. Originally a small flour-mill town, the area is now home to Union Craft Brewery, Taharka Brothers ice cream, and a handful of world-class restaurants. One of the newest on the scene is Birroteca, owned by Robbin Haas, one of *Food & Wine* magazine's top ten chefs in America in 1994.

Haas earned a reputation for being one of the founding fathers of New World Cuisine through his celebration of the flavors of South Florida. Additionally, he's opened restaurants that reflect his appreciation for the various culinary traditions of Asia and Europe. His first venture in Baltimore, Birroteca, stems from one of his real cooking loves—the rustic food of Italy.

The restaurant's name is meant to evoke an *enoteca*—an Italian wine bar. In Baltimore, a town that loves great beer, that translated to a concentration on local craft brews, like those from Evolution, Heavy Seas, Flying Dog, and nearby Union. But rather than serving burgers and buffalo wings, the expected accompaniments to all that beer, Birroteca offers pappardelle, polenta, and pizza.

There's been an artisan pizza explosion in Baltimore, and Birroteca's thin-crust, wood-fired pies are some of the best around. The toppings are inventive and include duck confit and fig-onion jam, roasted shrimp and burrata. There's also pasta, salumi, and appetizers like the best-selling, melt-in-your-mouth calamari alla plancha, which are prepared in a confit with garlic and capers before being given a quick sear on a cast-iron griddle.

Vegetables are given a lot of attention at Birroteca, and a vegetarian has no problem putting together a satisfying meal. People can't get enough of the crisp brussels sprouts with black garlic aioli. Another huge seller is the kale salad. "It's crazy the amount of kale we go through," says Haas.

Haas believes it's important to "keep it simple, keep it fresh, keep it local, and keep it approachable." Word of mouth originally brought customers to Birroteca, and this philosophy keeps them coming in. "We offer great service, good food, and an easy-to-get-to location, and we're happy that the community has accepted us."

It's the calamari, Chef.

SLOW COOKED CALAMARI "BIRROTECA STYLE"

(SERVES 4)

Slow-cooking the calamari in oil makes them exquisitely tender.

1½ pounds calamari, cleaned and cut into 2-inch rings

3 cloves garlic, crushed

1½ cups olive oil blend

2 teaspoons salt

¼ cup extra virgin olive oil

1 tablespoon minced garlic

1 lemon, quartered

2 tablespoons drained capers

2 tablespoons chopped fresh parsley

1 teaspoon kosher or sea salt

Preheat oven to 275°F.

Place the calamari, garlic, oil blend, and salt in an ovenproof casserole. Mix well. Cover with aluminum foil and braise for 2½ hours, or until the calamari are tender and soft.

Remove from oven and let cool. When cool, drain off oil. Calamari can be refrigerated at this point or used immediately.

When ready to serve, heat a 14-inch sauté pan over medium heat and add the extra virgin olive oil. Add the garlic and lemon and toast them in the oil. The garlic will turn light brown and start to smell nutty.

Place the calamari in the pan and cook until lightly golden brown.

Add the capers and parsley and, if desired, salt to taste and olive oil.

Serve immediately.

BLUE HILL TAVERN

938 S CONKLING STREET
BALTIMORE, MD 21224
(443) 388-9363
BLUEHILLTAVERN.COM
OWNERS: MEL CARTER, JIMMY STAVRAKIS, BRETT LOCKARD
CHEF: BRETT LOCKARD

Although Blue Hill Tavern is located in Brewer's Hill, in the shadow of the Mr. Boh sign, it's definitely not a brewpub. It's not really a tavern, either, nor is the hill blue. However, Blue Hill Tavern serves up good food in an attractive setting, and that's really all that counts, isn't it?

Chef and partner Brett Lockard graduated from the Culinary Institute of America and worked in New York, New Jersey, and his home state of Pennsylvania before opening Blue Hill Tavern with his best friend, Mel Carter, and business partner Jimmy Stavrakis. Together they created an elegantly appointed restaurant with dark wood floors, lots of windows, and several dining areas on two floors, including plenty of outdoor seating. The menu is classic American with a new slant.

"I feel some of the best dishes are traditional ones, with today's twists," says Lockard. How traditional? you ask. Pretty darn, as some of the best-selling dishes at the restaurant are the chateaubriand and the Wellington. And those twists? The chateaubriand is cooked *sous vide,* which makes it exceptionally tender. And the Wellington is made using only mushrooms, giving the formerly beefy dish new life as a vegetarian entree. There are some "world flavors" too, as in the Mediterranean-leaning skordalia and grilled halloumi cheese appetizers, and a global influence is definitely evident in the recipe Chef Lockard has provided here.

Barolo Braised Lamb Shanks
with Spiced Fregola
(SERVES 10)

Fregola is a small semolina-flour pasta from Sardinia. It's similar to couscous, but it is lightly toasted and has a rougher texture. If you can't find fregola in your local supermarket, try Israeli couscous or barley, cooked according to package directions before continuing with the rest of the recipe.

For the lamb shanks:

10 plum tomatoes
5 tablespoons olive oil (divided)
10 (1-pound) lamb shanks
Salt and pepper
1 cup diced celery
1 cup diced carrot
1 cup diced onion
2 cloves garlic
1½ tablespoons tomato paste
3 tablespoons all-purpose flour
2 cups Barolo or similar dry red wine
2 quarts brown veal stock or beef broth
1 bay leaf
2 sprigs thyme
½ sprig rosemary

For the spiced fregola:

16 ounces fregola
3 tablespoons olive oil
½ cup diced onion
½ cup diced parsnip
½ cup diced celery
⅛ teaspoon ground cardamom
⅛ teaspoon ground cloves
⅛ ground cinnamon
Salt and pepper

One day prior to serving: Preheat oven to 250°F. Cut the plum tomatoes into quarters and place them on a sheet pan lined with a wire rack. Drizzle the tomatoes with 2 tablespoons of the olive oil. Roast about 1 hour until they start to shrivel and become slightly sweet. Set aside to cool. When cool, peel and discard the skins. Reserve the tomatoes.

To make the lamb shanks: Preheat oven to 325°F. Season the lamb shanks with salt and pepper. Heat the remaining 3 tablespoons of oil on medium-high heat in a large dutch oven or stewpot. Add the shanks and sear on all sides until golden brown (you may need to do this in two batches). Remove and reserve.

Add the onions, celery, carrot, onion, and garlic to the pot and cook on medium heat until tender but not browned. Add the tomato paste and cook for 2 minutes more. Stir in the flour and cook for an additional 2 minutes. Add the red wine and bring to a simmer, then add the stock and bring back to the simmer. Return the reserved shanks to the pot along with any juices released from them. Season with the bay leaf, thyme, and rosemary, and bring everything again to a simmer.

Cover the pot and transfer to the oven. Cook for 1½–2 hours, until the meat is fork tender and starts to pull away from the bone.

Remove the lamb shanks to another pan and cover with a bit of the cooking liquid. Place the original pot on the stovetop and bring the cooking liquid up to a simmer. Check for seasoning and add salt and pepper. If the sauce seems thin, cook it for a while to reduce it. When the cooking liquid seems more like a sauce, add the reserved shanks and roasted tomatoes.

To make the fregola: Bring 8 quarts of water to a boil in a large pot. Add 1 teaspoon of salt. Cook the fregola until al dente. Drain and reserve.

Heat a large sauté pan over medium heat and add the oil. Cook the onion, parsnip, and celery for 3–5 minutes, until tender.

Add the spices. Cook about 1 minute. Add the drained fregola and cook 2 minutes more. Season with salt and pepper to taste.

To serve: Reheat shanks if not warm. Reheat fregola if not warm.

Divide the fregola among ten large pasta bowls. Place one shank in each bowl. Ladle over enough sauce to moisten the fregola.

The Brewer's Art

1106 N Charles Street
Baltimore, MD 21201
(410) 547-6925
thebrewersart.com
Owners: Tom Creegan, Volker Stewart
Chef: Ray Kumm

Set in a grand old Mount Vernon town house, the Brewer's Art is probably most famous as a brewpub producing delicious beers that can be found on tap and in bottles and cans all around town. *Esquire* magazine tagged them as Best Bar in America a few years back, and their rosemary garlic fries are a top seller. And yes, while we like to knock back a few Resurrections or Ozzys, we really go to the Brewer's Art to eat in the dining rooms behind the first-floor bar.

Chef Ray Kumm took over the kitchen at the Brewer's Art in 2012. He started his cooking career when he took a restaurant job while pursuing a degree in English. Determining that the pace and pressure to perform on a daily basis would be more interesting than an office job, Kumm went to work at a French restaurant and has

"learned by doing ever since." This dedication is especially evident in his mastery of proteins.

"I like to cook food that is creative and different while trying to remain grounded in classic European flavor profiles and culinary approaches, favoring French, northern Italian, German, and Slavic." At the Brewer's Art this translates to a focus on creating interpretations of classic German, Austrian, and Belgian food to match with their European-style beers, but it also includes interesting pan-European creations like the caponata pierogi on last summer's menu. There's also a focus on more exotic (at least to Baltimore) meats, like pheasant and goat, as evidenced by the recipe Chef Kumm has shared with us.

Wagon Wheel Ranch Goat Goulash
with Short Grain Rice & Cherry Glen Crottin

(SERVES 10, WITH MEAT LEFT OVER)

"This dish is inspired by a regional Croatian specialty in which slow braised veal is stirred into risotto for a hearty and warming meal. Instead of veal, we use young, flavorful goats raised in Mount Airy. Instead of Arborio rice, we use a shorter grain called Vialone Nano because it has a more supple texture that matches better with the meaty ragù. Instead of using a more typical cheese like Parmesan, we use an aged goat's milk crottin from Cherry Glen Farms in Boyds, Maryland, to reinforce the flavor of the goat. At the restaurant we get two whole goats at a time (about 90 pounds), breaking them down completely, using the carcasses for stock and reserving the loins for another purpose. This recipe is scaled down significantly for the home chef. You can always scale down the rice further, but the goulash needs to be made in at least this quantity, so you could freeze a portion of it for another day."

For the goat and marinade:

1 leg fresh local goat (approximately 8 pounds)
1 tablespoon minced garlic
1 teaspoon sweet paprika
1 tablespoon Aleppo pepper
1 teaspoon ground toasted fennel seed
2 tablespoons kosher salt
1 cup olive oil

For the stock:

2 large carrots, peeled and chopped
3 stalks celery
1 Spanish onion, peeled and halved
4 cups pureed San Marzano tomatoes
2 bay leaves

For the rice:

1 cup finely diced Spanish onion
½ cup olive oil
4 cups Vialone Nano rice
Remaining stock, plus up to 2 cups of chicken
    stock, if needed
2 tablespoons unsalted butter
¾ cups grated Cherry Glen Farms crottin
Celery leaves, for garnish

To make the goat and marinade: Remove all meat from the bone and cut it into 1-inch cubes. Reserve the bone for the stock.

In a large ziplock bag, combine the goat meat, garlic, paprika, Aleppo pepper, fennel seed, salt, and olive oil. Press as much air as possible out of the bag, then seal and refrigerate overnight.

To make the stock: Preheat oven to 350°F.

Place the leg bone, carrots, celery, and onion in a roasting pan and roast until the bone is browned. Place in your largest stockpot with the tomatoes, bay leaves, and 2 gallons of water over high heat. Once the stock is at a simmer, turn the heat all the way down and allow to reduce by half. Strain the stock and refrigerate until ready to use.

To cook the goat: In a large dutch oven or similarly sized heavy-bottomed pot, combine the meat in its marinade and 1 gallon of the strained goat stock over medium heat. Once the pot has come to a simmer, reduce heat to low and cook until the meat is very tender and the sauce has become thick, 3–4 hours. Remove from heat and season with salt.

Cool completely, preferably overnight so that the flavors of the ragù have a chance to meld.

To make the rice and complete the dish: Put the remaining goat stock in one pot over medium heat and chicken stock in another pot and bring both to a simmer. Reduce heat to low.

In a very large heavy-bottomed pot, sweat the onions in the olive oil. Once translucent, add the rice and toast it in the pan, stirring constantly with a wooden spoon for 90 seconds.

Add 1½ cups of the hot goat stock. Continue stirring. Once most of the liquid has been absorbed, continue adding hot stock 1 cup at a time, stirring constantly. Keep tasting the rice, checking the texture. You are looking for a texture that is easy to bite into, but still firm enough that it won't become a porridge by the time it is finished. Use the chicken stock if the goat stock runs out before the proper texture is achieved.

Once this texture has been reached, stir in 4 cups of the goulash, the butter, and 1 cup of cheese. Beat the mixture vigorously for about 30 seconds. Check for seasoning and serve immediately, garnishing with the remaining cheese and the celery leaves.

BALTIMORE RESTAURANTS IN THE MOVIES

Baltimore is a moviemaker's paradise. Or so it seems. Dozens of movies and television shows have been made in Charm City, and that's not counting those in John Waters's oeuvre. We've hosted celebs from George Clooney to Julia Roberts, from Keanu Reeves to Brad Pitt.

You want a substitute for DC? Baltimore's your place. You want quirky and urban? Baltimore's your place. And it's not just the monument-filled streets of the Monumental City that find their way onto film, but also a fair number of local restaurants, which may or may not be playing themselves.

For example, in the Meg Ryan–Tom Hanks vehicle *Sleepless in Seattle,* there's a scene between Meg and her on-screen BFF Rosie O'Donnell that takes place in the old lunchroom at the Woman's Industrial Exchange. The bar fight scene in Keanu Reeves's *The Replacements* takes place in a South Baltimore restaurant called Little Havana.

Two long-running television shows about the work of various Baltimore policemen, *Homicide* and *The Wire,* had regular scenes in local restaurants. Jimmy's, a little diner on Broadway in Fells Point, served as the backdrop for many a breakfast meeting on *Homicide,* and the Waterfront Tavern, around the corner, was the location for the bar owned by Detectives Bayliss, Lewis, and Munch. *The Wire* filmed scenes all over the place, including Chaps Pit Beef, the Brewer's Art, the Wine Market, and the Water Street location of Ruth's Chris.

Currently the Netflix original series *House of Cards* is filming in Baltimore. This time the city is standing in for Washington, DC. While Freddy's BBQ Joint is a completely fictitious restaurant filmed in an abandoned building on Greenmount Avenue, other scenes have been shot in the very real Tio Pepe, Wit & Wisdom, and Red Maple, all posing as DC-area restaurants.

Cafe Gia

410 S High Street
Baltimore, MD 21202
(410) 685-6727
CAFEGIAS.COM
OWNER: GIA BLATTERMAN
CHEF: GIANFRANCO FRACASSETTI

Most of Little Italy is a warren of narrow streets lined with brick rowhouses. Some continue to be occupied by generations of Italian families, while others have been converted to restaurants. If you wander down to the end of South High Street, where it meets Eastern Avenue, you may feel transported to a small village in Sicily. The quaint, brightly colored storefront that is Cafe Gia is carefully decorated to elicit that very response.

But this conscious effort to depict a rustic Sicilian trattoria in the heart of Baltimore was not merely a commercial design choice. Rather it is a sincere reflection of the family's heritage. The Aquia family came to Baltimore from Sicily in 1953. As matriarch Giovanna puts it, "At a time when no one liked to move around, our family traveled thirty-five hundred miles, and we haven't moved two hundred feet since." Four generations of her family have lived in Little Italy, and Gia Blatterman wanted to own a restaurant that honored their long association not only with the neighborhood but with their Sicilian homeland. She now runs the tiny eatery with Chef Gianfranco Fracassetti in the kitchen—both at the restaurant and at home. Owner and chef are sweethearts and have a young daughter together.

While Gia's family hailed from Sicily, Fracassetti was born in Lombardy, pretty much at the opposite end of Italy. He attended culinary school at the age of fourteen, following in the footsteps of his older brother. After cooking at a few local Baltimore restaurants, Chef Gianfranco came to work at Cafe Gia in 2009. His specialty is homemade stuffed pastas, and he enjoys creating new sauces to complement them. His favorite item on the Cafe Gia menu, a signature of his created some years ago, is the Fettuccine Lucia, which was renamed after his daughter (who is also a fan). The homemade black pepper fettuccine tossed with house-made chicken sausage, arugula, red grapes, and goat cheese in a delicate wine sauce has a lovely sweetness and a light peppery kick. If you can't make it to Little Italy, the recipe follows so that you can try it at home.

Fettuccine Lucia

(SERVES 4–6)

1 pound fettuccine (black pepper infused
   if you can find it)
1 cup olive oil
1 pound Italian chicken sausage, removed
   from casing
1 cup white cooking wine
1 tablespoon minced garlic
2½ cups whole red grapes
½ pound fresh, creamy goat cheese
1 bunch arugula
Parmigiano Reggiano cheese (optional)

In a large pot of salted water, cook the fettuccine al dente. Drain and reserve.

Meanwhile, warm the olive oil in a large sauté pan over medium heat. Add the chicken sausage, using a wooden spoon to break the meat into smaller pieces. Add the white wine and garlic. Simmer until the sausage is lightly browned. (Although it is cooked through, chicken sausage tends to appear pink in certain areas.)

Add the grapes, 2 tablespoons of the goat cheese, the arugula, and the cooked fettuccine. Using tongs, mix the ingredients together gently until the pasta is coated.

Place the pasta in a bowl and crumble the remainder of the goat cheese on top. Add freshly grated Parmigiano Reggiano if desired.

Chazz: A Bronx Original

1415 Aliceanna Street
Baltimore, MD 21231
(410) 522-5511
chazzbronxoriginal.com
Owners: Sergio Vitale, Alessandro Vitale
Chef: Sergio Vitale

When actor Chazz Palminteri was in Baltimore with his one-man show, *A Bronx Tale,* he tried a couple of local Italian restaurants before he landed at Aldo's. He found their simplest of dishes, a linguine marinara, so perfect that he dined there every night for the rest of the show's run. Soon he became fast friends with the owners, the Vitale family. Palminteri had always wanted to be in the restaurant business, so when he discovered that brothers Sergio and Alessandro Vitale were working on a pizza concept, he jumped at the chance to join forces with them. And Chazz: A Bronx Original was born.

Chazz, like Aldo's, is an Italian restaurant, but that's where the similarities end. Aldo's is a quiet, elegant oasis in the city, but Chazz has a busier, more casual vibe. Bars dominate the space: the pizza bar, where diners can sit and watch their pies being prepared and baked; the mozzarella bar where the cheeses and salumi are displayed; and the wood-framed cocktail bar that takes up a good part of the room. Depending on

where one sits, Chazz can seem like several different restaurants. And if you score the singular cushy booth at the back of the dining room, you feel like a VIP. It's Chazz's booth, after all, and yes, he does visit Baltimore more frequently than you'd think.

As with Aldo's, Sergio Vitale runs the kitchen. At Chazz he still insists on making practically everything in-house, from the pizzas and pastas to the fresh fruit juices for the cocktails. About the only thing Sergio doesn't make himself is the burrata, an almost evilly luscious cheese made with mozzarella and cream that has become a runaway hit at Chazz, starring in the Caprese salad and the best-selling Margherita pizza.

Those pizzas are Bronx style, by the way, baked in a custom-made coal-fired oven that blazes up to 1,000 degrees and can turn out one of the restaurant's delicious red clam pies in ninety seconds. Pizzas are a top seller, and it's not unusual to see tables with two or three pies balancing on special wire racks. We're rather fond of the veal meatball pizza. That meatball can also be found in a sandwich, and as a supersize version served with whipped ricotta and sausage "gravy." Here's the recipe, so you can try it for yourself.

VEAL MEATBALLS

(SERVES 4–6)

There's a debate as to whether a panade is necessary to make a meatball. A panade is made with stale bread cubes softened by soaking in liquid and serves to add moisture to meatballs. Chef Aldo Vitale of Baltimore's Aldo's doesn't use a panade; instead, he uses dry bread crumbs. But using only bread crumbs can lead to a dry meatball if experienced hands do not make the mixture. This recipe employs a panade, which can ensure a moist meatball by pros and novices alike.

3 cups day-old Italian bread, crust removed and
    discarded, cut into 1-inch cubes
1 cup whole milk
¾ pound ground veal
½ pound ground beef
½ pound ground pork
3 eggs, beaten
4 large cloves garlic, finely minced
1 cup grated pecorino cheese
¼ cup finely chopped Italian flat-leaf parsley
½ teaspoon kosher salt, or to taste
½ teaspoon ground white pepper
4–5 cups of your favorite tomato sauce or
    ragù Bolognese
½ cup chicken stock

In a shallow bowl, soak the bread cubes in milk to cover for a few minutes. Drain the bread cubes and squeeze with your fingers to press out the excess moisture.

In a large bowl, combine the drained bread cubes, ground meats, eggs, garlic, cheese, parsley, and seasonings and mix with your hands to incorporate them all well.

At this point, you can test the seasoning by heating 1 tablespoon olive oil in a nonstick sauté pan over medium-high heat. Take 1–2 tablespoons of the meatball mixture, form a flat patty, and cook the patty in the hot olive oil for 2–3 minutes on each side until browned and cooked through. Taste for seasoning. If more garlic or salt is needed, you can add it now before rolling the meatballs.

With wet hands, form the mixture into 14–16 meatballs. Roll them with some pressure to compress the meat into perfectly round balls that will not fall apart while cooking. If the mixture sticks to your hands, dab a finger or two into a small bowl of room-temperature water while rolling. Reserve all the meatballs on a baking sheet.

In a large stockpot, heat your chosen sauce along with the chicken stock over medium heat until the mixture reaches a light simmer. Gently add the meatballs one by one, ensuring that they are all covered by sauce. Cook at a light simmer for 17–23 minutes, or until the meatballs are cooked through.

CITY CAFE

1001 CATHEDRAL STREET
BALTIMORE, MD 21201
(410) 539-4252
CITYCAFEBALTIMORE.COM
OWNERS: GINO CARDINALE, BRUCE BODIE
CHEF: JARED RHINE

City Cafe has a bit of a split personality. On the one hand, the Mount Vernon establishment offers a cafe serving Zeke's coffee, pastries, smoothies, and a full lunch menu. On the other hand, their restaurant offers American cuisine featuring seasonal local ingredients. And let's not forget the sophisticated bar area. All three are sleek and handsome, promoting a convivial and casual atmosphere that allows patrons to focus on the friendly environment and delicious food.

The creator of that delicious food is Jared Rhine, who worked previously in Florida and his home state of Pennsylvania before coming to Baltimore and working at Canton's Field House and the late Della Notte in Little Italy. Chef Rhine has a background in both Italian and French cuisine; both influences, along with some other ethnic touches, can be seen in his menu of seasonal American cuisine. "I love the structure of French cooking and its definitive techniques. I also love Italian cooking's simplicity of flavors and the huge emphasis on using local products. But I also love the spices and flavors of Indian and other Asian cuisines." He's also a fan of cooking *sous vide,* a technique by which proteins are cooked as close to perfectly as they'll ever be. The process can "impart so much flavor to a very underused or underappreciated piece of meat, fish, vegetable, or even eggs." Not that something like prime rib will ever be underappreciated, but a trip through the immersion circulator turns City Cafe's version into something special.

About half of Chef Rhine's menu is made up of small plates, sharing plates, and a selection of oysters—perfect for a bite to eat before hitting the clubs. There's also a light fare section, which in the case of City Cafe includes salads and sandwiches, and a selection of hearty, full-on entrees. The restaurant also serves an amazing selection of breakfast and lunch items. With the three squares, coffee, and sexy cocktails at City Cafe, we're surprised that no one has tried to live there.

SEARED SEA SCALLOPS WITH CAULIFLOWER "STEAK," BEER BATTERED ASPARAGUS "FRIES" & FOUR CITRUS REDUCTION

(SERVES 2)

If you omit the scallops, the rest of the dish makes a fine vegetarian entree.

For the asparagus "fries":

3 ounces mint leaves
3 ounces fresh ginger, peeled and roughly chopped
2 cloves garlic, peeled
¼ shallot
2 teaspoons pink peppercorns
1 teaspoon sea salt
½ teaspoon freshly ground black pepper
¼ cup white wine
2–4 cups flour
16 ounces lager, preferably Stella Artois
1 pound asparagus
3 quarts vegetable oil

For the cauliflower "steak":

1 head cauliflower
Softened unsalted butter
Salt and pepper

For the citrus reduction:

½ cup granulated sugar
⅛ cup water
¼ cup sherry
½ cup grapefruit juice
½ cup orange juice
½ cup lemon juice
½ cup lime juice
1 tablespoon unsalted butter

For the scallops:

12 fresh sea scallops (1 pound)
Sea salt
Freshly ground black pepper
Oil for frying

To make the asparagus fries: Put the mint, ginger, garlic, shallot, pink peppercorns, salt, and black pepper in a food processor and, slowly adding the wine, process until smooth.

Transfer the puree to a mixing bowl and add 2 cups of flour and half the beer. Stir in the remaining beer and as much flour as necessary to make a semi-thick batter.

Cut the asparagus into 1-inch lengths. Heat the oil in a large, heavy, steep-sided pot until it reaches about 350°F. Dredge the asparagus pieces in batter, shaking off the excess. Fry in the preheated oil until golden brown. Drain on paper-towel-lined plates.

To make the cauliflower "steak": Preheat oven to 325°F.

Trim the stem of the cauliflower, then cut the head down the middle through the stem. Slice one ¾-inch-thick "steak" from each half, reserving the remaining cauliflower for another use. Rub one side of each steak with softened butter and season with salt and pepper.

Preheat an ovenproof sauté pan over medium heat and add the steaks, butter side down. Place the pan in the preheated oven and roast for fifteen minutes, until golden brown and fork tender.

To make the citrus reduction: Combine the sugar and water in a saucepan and cook over low heat until the sugar turns a medium amber color, about 8–10 minutes.

Remove the pan from the heat and carefully pour in the sherry. The mixture will bubble and steam, so use caution. Put the pan back on the heat, add the citrus juices, and stir until the liquids are incorporated into the caramel. Cook until the mixture coats the back of a spoon. Stir in the butter.

To make the scallops: Pat the scallops dry with paper towels and lightly season both sides with sea salt and black pepper.

Preheat a sauté pan and add 2 tablespoons of oil. When the oil is hot, add the scallops and sear on one side. Turn the scallops and sear the second side. Turn off heat and allow scallops to rest until they are slightly translucent at the center.

To plate: Place a cauliflower steak at the center of each plate. Arrange scallops on top, and pile asparagus alongside. Drizzle citrus reduction over the scallops and asparagus.

CLEMENTINE

5402 HARFORD ROAD
BALTIMORE, MD 21214
(410) 444-1497
BMORECLMENTINE.COM
OWNERS: CHEF WINSTON BLICK, CRISTIN DADANT

Winston Blick wasn't sure what he was getting himself into when he and his wife, Cristin Dadant, decided to open a restaurant a few blocks from their house in Hamilton. Hamilton was never known as a hotbed of fine cuisine, but over the past handful of years this Baltimore City neighborhood and its sister to the south, Lauraville, have become home to several notable restaurants, Clementine being one of them.

Farm-to-table has become the major trend in the culinary world, and Blick and Dadant show an obsessive devotion to it. Not only do they update their menu daily based on the freshest ingredients available, they also make their own charcuterie, pickled vegetables, dressings, sauces, and jams right on the premises. "Our food is honest. Our approach is honest," says Blick. Diners can usually expect to find such items as chicken

liver pâté, ham, and various types of sausage on the menu. The proteins are paired with a combination of mustards and condiments specially concocted by the chef. But lest you think the menu is all pork snouts all the time, we'd like to assure you there are also juicy burgers made with a special in-house grind (chuck, sirloin, brisket, and short rib), mighty fine duck nachos, and even scrumptious vegetarian-friendly dishes. Oh, and the world's best coconut cake, made by Blick's own mama.

Clementine's commitment to locally produced food does not stop at the restaurant. Down the street is the Green Onion, a grocery store that they own with partner Richard Marsiglia. There you can find locally grown produce, locally raised meats, and locally made products like Zeke's Coffee and artisan jams and jellies.

"I like the sentimentality of food. I like things that remind me of other things, of my family, of the giant garden we had when I was growing up. Of hunting and crabbing. That translates to my cooking in that I'm always looking to remind you of some good time in your past."

Chicken Liver Pâté

(SERVES 16–20)

Pâté is served cold, and cold diminishes flavor, so remember to season aggressively!

1 pound unsalted butter

½ pound good-quality bacon, chopped roughly

3 cloves garlic, peeled

2 shallots, roughly chopped

1 pound chicken livers, rinsed

1 ounce bourbon or rye whiskey, or wine or liqueur of your choice

4–5 tablespoons maple syrup, or to taste

Salt and pepper, to taste

In a large saucepan, melt the butter over medium heat. Add the bacon, garlic, and shallots, and poach until soft.

Add the livers to the pan and poach until they are only slightly pink inside.

Remove the pan from the heat and allow the contents to cool to about 100–120°F. When cool, pour into a food processor. Add the liquor and maple syrup and process until completely combined.

Season with salt and pepper to taste and allow to cool completely before serving.

DONNA'S

VILLAGE OF CROSS KEYS
5100 FALLS ROAD
BALTIMORE, MD 21210
(410) 532-7611
DONNAS.COM/CROSSKEYS
OWNERS: DONNA CRIVELLO,
ALAN HIRSCH
CHEF: IAN STANFORD

Donna Crivello and business partner Alan Hirsch opened their original coffee bar on the corner of Madison and Charles Streets in the early 1990s. "After traveling independently to Italy, France, and the West Coast, returning with ideas for warm, inviting, casual cafes that were open all day, we agreed that we wanted a place like that in Baltimore." And Donna's was born. It was a terrific place to stop for a giant cappuccino or latte—both beverages still pretty new and exciting here in Baltimore—and to nibble a pastry or something more substantial while settled in for some people-watching at one of the popular sidewalk tables.

The Mount Vernon neighborhood was perfumed daily by the scent of Donna's roasted vegetables—a mélange of white and sweet potatoes, beets, eggplant, and onions—which formed the basis for both a popular salad and a sandwich. Soon Donna's branched out into other locations, including Harborplace, Charles Village, and the Baltimore Museum of Art (BMA). Today Donna's is down to two locations— Charles Village, near Johns Hopkins University, and the Village of Cross Keys, a planned community in the north of Baltimore City. Sadly, the original Mount Vernon location was lost to fire.

The chef at Donna's Cross Keys is Ian Stanford, who worked at Donna's at the BMA as "a budding chef just out of school." After a handful of years working in other restaurants, he returned to Donna's. Originally from the tiny town of Laytonsville (population 353) in Montgomery County, Chef Stanford credits his favorite childhood television show, *Three's Company,* with his decision to become a chef. The character of Jack Tripper made cooking seem so fun, Ian decided to go to culinary school. Today, he says, he's "trying my hardest to deliver creative, attractive, and honest food and trying my best not to get caught up in the trends of the day."

Donna Crivello says, "Ian masterfully prepares things that seem simple, like a soup, which he layers with flavors and textures." While he does stick to the restaurant's strong Mediterranean leanings, his interest in South American and Asian cuisines comes through in specials and seasonal menu additions.

TOMATO & RED PEPPER BISQUE

(SERVES 6–8)

Donna's tomato bisque is by far one of the most popular soups they serve. Here some roasted red bell peppers have been added to the original recipe. Not only do they add a level of flavor, but the oil from the peppers emulsifies the soup once it is pureed. You'll find it rich as is, but you could still add a bit of cream for an even richer flavor. Serve with grilled cheese panini cut into small triangles.

For the roasted peppers:

3 large red bell peppers
Salt and pepper, to taste

For the bisque:

1 red onion, diced
4 cloves garlic, chopped
1–2 tablespoons olive oil

½ cup red wine
1 teaspoon dried basil
4 pounds ripe tomatoes, peeled, diced, and cooked, or 3 (14-ounce) cans
1–2 cups vegetable stock or water
10–12 fresh basil leaves
½–1 cup heavy cream (optional)
Grated Parmesan or Romano cheese

To roast the peppers: Cut the peppers in half lengthwise and remove the stems and seeds. Place the pepper halves, cut side down, on a foil-lined and oiled cookie sheet. Sprinkle with salt and pepper. Roast for 25 minutes or until the flesh is tender and the skin is blistered.

Cover the pan with foil and allow the peppers to cool. When cool enough to handle, rub off the skins. The peppers are ready to use.

To make the bisque: In a large pot, gently sauté the onion and garlic in oil over medium heat. Add the wine and dried basil. Simmer for about 10 minutes. Add the tomatoes, roasted red peppers, and stock. Simmer for 30–45 minutes. Stack the basil leaves and slice them thinly into a chiffonade. Add a handful to the soup pot.

Puree the mixture with an immersion blender or standard blender. Taste and add more salt and/or basil if needed. Slowly pour in the cream (if using), stirring until you achieve the desired flavor and color.

Serve in large warmed bowls. Top with grated Parmesan cheese and the remaining fresh basil. Panini triangles make a nice accompaniment.

SICILIAN CAULIFLOWER SALAD
(SERVES 6–8)

This salad is one of Donna's current favorite dishes. Great as a side with grilled fish or poultry, it can be made into a main dish by adding some chickpeas, couscous, or pasta.

1 small head cauliflower
1 tablespoon olive oil
Salt and pepper, to taste
1–2 tablespoons lemon juice
1–2 cloves garlic, finely minced
2–3 tablespoons golden raisins
2–3 teaspoons toasted pine nuts
2 ripe tomatoes, diced
12 kalamata olives, pitted, roughly chopped
20 leaves fresh mint, torn into small pieces
1 teaspoon fresh oregano, finely chopped
1 teaspoon red pepper flakes (optional)

Preheat oven to 375°F.

Trim the leaves from the cauliflower. Cut into florets by trimming pieces from the stalk to release whole little clusters. Toss these pieces with olive oil, salt, and pepper. Place on a baking pan and bake for about 15 minutes, or until just tender and slightly browned on the edges. Allow to cool a bit before proceeding.

Toss the cauliflower florets in a bowl with the lemon juice (1 teaspoon white balsamic vinegar can be used in place of some of the lemon juice), garlic, raisins, pine nuts, diced tomatoes, olives, and fresh herbs. Taste for seasoning and add salt and pepper and optional red pepper flakes.

Allow salad to rest for at least 30 minutes and up to 2 hours for flavors to meld.

Refrigerate until ready to serve. Will hold for 1–2 days, but the texture of the cauliflower will soften.

DONNA'S DARK CHOCOLATE SORBETTO
(SERVES 12)

With a bit of experimenting, Donna came up with a chocolate sorbetto that is very rich, but also low in fat and dairy free. It's a new favorite dessert at Cross Keys, where guests who request the recipe are surprised that it is so easy to make.

2 cups granulated sugar
1½ cups dark, Dutch-process, unsweetened cocoa
3¼ cups hot water
1 teaspoon vanilla

In a medium saucepan, whisk together the sugar and cocoa. Gradually add the hot water and vanilla, being careful to eliminate any lumps. Cook over high heat until the mixture begins to boil. Reduce heat and simmer for about 10 minutes or until the mixture thickens a bit and is smooth and silky.

Allow the mixture to cool in the pan before pouring into a 4 x 8-inch plastic or stainless steel container.

Freeze for at least 8 hours or overnight. When it is frozen, cover with plastic wrap or a lid until ready to use.

Scoop into small martini glasses. Serve immediately.

Fleet Street Kitchen

1012 Fleet Street
Baltimore, MD 21202
(410) 244-5830
FLEETSTREETKITCHEN.COM
Owner: The Bagby Group
Chef: Chris Amendola
Pastry Chef: Bettina Perry

The industrial exterior of Fleet Street Kitchen, with its corrugated tin awning and brick fascia, might suggest a cramped restaurant with rickety wooden chairs and repurposed wall art. Inside, however, the crystal chandeliers and comfy banquettes let diners know that they are in for a more elegant experience. In fact, this contrast in design matches the culinary philosophy of a restaurant where classic cooking techniques are melded with a modern nose-to-tail approach. Chief Operations Officer Chris Becker and Executive Chef Chris Amendola have concocted a menu that has a particular focus on charcuterie and offal. Also, they source much of the menu's ingredients from their own Cunningham Farms in Cockeysville. In addition to herbs, vegetables, and greens, the farm raises pigs and chickens for the restaurant.

"Flavor isn't just built in the kitchen, but in the whole growing process," says Chef Amendola. "Cooking and eating are about bringing out the natural flavors of incredible local products that we are connected to either by growing them ourselves or having relationships with those that grow them."

Growing up in St. Augustine, Florida, Chef Amendola developed a passion for the culinary arts while accompanying his mother to work at a local restaurant. Fascinated with the dynamics of the kitchen, he was determined to be a chef. His formal training came from the Southeast Institute of Culinary Arts in St. Augustine, but he refined his craft under Chef Todd English at bluezoo in Orlando and with Chef Sean Brock. He learned quite a bit about farming as well, working at Thackeray Farms in Wadmalaw Island, South Carolina, and working closely with the team at Blue Hill Farm while at Blue Hill restaurant in New York. Embracing the locally driven, seasonal ethic of Fleet Street Kitchen, originally set forth by Bagby executive chef Chris Becker, Amendola seeks to craft elegant contemporary American dishes that highlight the very best ingredients.

The team's desire to use the entire animal in their cooking is well reflected in their charcuterie, which at any time may include lardo, pork rillettes, liverwurst, and pork rind. There's even a Pig Face and Pickles menu that offers ears and snouts. Lest diners think

that they might be greeted with a plate of food from Granny Clampett's kitchen, be assured that all the dishes are treated with the level of care and sophistication you would expect in a fine dining establishment. The crisp pork belly, for example, is complemented with a poached egg, smoked maple glaze, and buttered toast powder.

To pair with the restaurant's cuisine, Beverage Director Tim Riley and Sommelier Philip Lucas curate an impressive five-thousand-bottle wine cellar, a craft beer menu, and a list of artisan cocktails that are also crafted in-house using ingredients from Cunningham Farms and local sources.

The blend of old and new is, for Chef Amendola, part of what makes the Baltimore culinary scene so exciting. "I think it's fantastic, really collaborative and creative. While Baltimore still has its culinary traditions, there are a lot of people who are doing some really cool things with those traditions and making them fresh and new."

CRISPY PORK BELLY WITH POACHED EGG
& SMOKED MAPLE GLAZE

(SERVES 2)

This specific recipe makes two servings, which require only a few ounces of pork belly. But we think there can't be enough pork belly in our diets, so why not cook up a whole slab and use it in other ways? Having more available also makes it easy to increase the recipe servings from two to twenty and any number in between.

For the pork belly:

4 cups water

1 cup brown sugar

1 cup kosher salt

2 tablespoons fennel seed

2 tablespoons yellow mustard seed

5 sprigs fresh thyme

1 head of garlic, cut in half crosswise

5 sprigs fresh tarragon

3 pounds pork belly, in a single slab

6 cups lard

For the buttered toast powder:

4 slices sourdough bread

Butter

Salt and pepper, to taste

For the smoked maple glaze:

1 cup maple syrup

4 tablespoons unsalted butter

Dash of liquid smoke

For the eggs:

1 free-range egg per serving

White vinegar

For assembly:

1 (¼-pound) slice confit pork belly, cut in half

4 tablespoons buttered toast powder

2 large eggs

2 ounces smoked maple glaze

To make the pork belly: Begin the preparation at least 2 days ahead of time: Combine all ingredients except the pork belly and lard in a medium pot and bring to a boil. Stir until the salt and sugar are dissolved.

Pour the brine into a container large enough to hold both the pork and the brine. Refrigerate until the brine is completely cold, then submerge the pork belly and refrigerate.

After 2 days, take the pork out of the brine. Rinse the pork and allow to air dry for 30 minutes.

Preheat the oven to 200°F.

Place the pork belly in a lidded, oven-safe cooking pot that is just slightly wider than the pork but deep enough that the meat can be submerged in lard. Cover the belly with enough lard to cover it by ½ inch or so.

Heat the pot on the stovetop until the lard reaches about 190°F. Cover the pot and transfer it to the preheated oven. Cook the pork for 4–6 hours, until tender. Remove from the oven

and allow to cool to room temperature. Store, refrigerated and covered in lard, for up to 1 week.

To make the buttered toast powder: Preheat oven to 250°F.

Toast the slices of bread, then spread both sides with butter. Place the buttered toast on a baking sheet and place in the oven. Bake for about 20 minutes, turning occasionally, until totally dehydrated. Grind the bread to a powder in a food processor.

To make the smoked maple glaze: Gently warm the maple syrup, then whisk in the butter until completely melted. Stir in the liquid smoke. (If you have a cold smoker, smoke the syrup for 20 minutes before adding the butter, and omit the liquid smoke.)

To poach the eggs: Bring a pot of water to a boil and add a splash of white vinegar. While the water is boiling, stir the water in a circular motion, then crack an egg into the center of the whirlpool. Gently stir the water to keep the egg moving.

Remove each egg after 4 minutes and drain on paper towels until ready to serve.

To assemble the dish: Sear the pork belly in a hot sauté pan for 4–5 minutes on each side.

Place a piece of pork belly on each of two plates, make a nice pile of the toast powder right next to the pork belly, and place an egg on top of the powder. Spoon the sauce on and around the pork belly.

The Food Market

1017 W 36TH STREET
BALTIMORE, MD 21211
(410) 366-0606
THEFOODMARKETBALTIMORE.COM
OWNERS: CHEF CHAD GAUSS, ELAN KOTZ

The Food Market is a brilliant name for a restaurant, particularly one that occupies what was once an old grocery store. It is a little hard to imagine, however, that this large modern space with a bustling open kitchen at the back was once filled with shelves of tinned meats and laundry detergent. Rather it seems like this busy eatery, on a stretch of Hampden's 36th Street popularly known as "the Avenue," has always been there, serving up modern comfort food—and food you didn't realize was comfort food until you tried it, like crispy lobster fingers or a club sandwich bursting with shrimp salad and a crab cake as well as the customary B, L, and T.

When Chef-Owner Chad Gauss was a teen, he knew he was born to cook professionally. "I have cooked anywhere someone would let me," says Gauss, who received his degree from the Baltimore International College and has worked at notable local restaurants like Christopher Daniel in Timonium and City Cafe in Mount Vernon. His work at City Cafe, by the way, earned him Best New Chef accolades from *Baltimore* magazine in 2010. In early 2012 he left that restaurant to open his own venture in Hampden, a restaurant-friendly neighborhood he feels is "on the right track" culinarily.

Gauss says, "The Baltimore food scene is just about having fun. It's great that chefs of our city are more friendly than competitive." It's a sentiment we've heard from other local chefs as well. And Gauss is certainly having fun with his collection of "little," "small," and "big" plates. At the Food Market he tries to "please as many people as possible" by cooking "anything that makes people smile." Dishes are familiar, with a twist, like the buttery Amish soft pretzels with a beer cheese fondue that's so good, we find ourselves dipping everything we order into it, or the popcorn served with grated cheese and truffle oil. His fried chicken is some of the best around, and the bread pudding, a creation by James Jennings, Gauss's chef de cuisine, is a perfect sweet ending to a meal at the Food Market.

Fried Chicken

(SERVES 4 IF USING BONE-IN CHICKEN, 10 IF USING BONELESS)

"Serve this crunchy chicken with gravy, hot sauce, or mornay sauce (a white sauce with cheese). This is great for chicken and waffles, with biscuits, poached eggs, or mashed potatoes and stewed green beans! I like it with hot sauce and watermelon!"

For the brine:

1 quart water
¼ cup salt
4 bay leaves
1 tablespoon ground black pepper
5 cloves garlic
3 sprigs thyme
4 ounces dark brown sugar
32 ounces National Bohemian beer
4 pounds chicken (boneless breasts or
   a combination of bone-in pieces)

For the seasoned flour:

3⅓ cups all-purpose flour
2¼ ounces cornstarch
1½ teaspoons onion powder
1½ teaspoons garlic powder
1 tablespoon salt
¾ teaspoon white pepper

For assembly:

Oil for frying
1 quart buttermilk

To make the brine: Place the water, salt, bay leaves, pepper, garlic, and thyme in a large pot with a lid. Bring the mixture to a boil, then remove the pot from the heat. Stir in the sugar and the beer. Allow to cool completely.

Place the chicken pieces in the brine and refrigerate for 24 hours, or at least overnight.

To make the seasoned flour: Combine all dry ingredients in a large bowl. Whisk well so there are no lumps. Transfer half of the seasoned flour to a separate large bowl.

To fry the chicken: Add oil to your deep fryer according to the manufacturer's instructions. Or add about 3 inches of oil to a deep, heavy pan with straight sides (oil should not come up more than halfway).

Preheat the oil to 300°F.

Remove the chicken from the brine and pat dry.

Dredge a few pieces of chicken at a time in the seasoned flour. Dip them next in the buttermilk, then in the second bowl of seasoned flour. Make sure the chicken pieces are completely coated.

Fry the chicken a few pieces at a time for about 12 minutes, or until the chicken floats. Do not crowd the pan, or the oil will cool down and the chicken will be greasy.

Remove the cooked chicken to paper-towel-lined plates to drain.

Heath Bar Bread Pudding

(SERVES 8–10)

5 eggs
1 quart heavy cream
½ cup sugar
1½ ounces Irish Cream liqueur, preferably Bailey's
2 teaspoons vanilla
12 ounces fresh white bread, cut into large dice
1 cup Heath chocolate toffee bits, plus
   more for garnish
1 (14-ounce) can sweetened condensed milk
Freshly whipped cream

Preheat oven to 350°F.

In a large bowl, whisk together the eggs, cream, sugar, liqueur, and vanilla. Add the diced bread and Heath bits and allow to sit until the bread is well soaked, about 30 minutes.

Pour the mixture into a greased 9 x 13 x 2-inch baking pan and cover the pan with foil. Bake for 30 minutes. Remove the foil and bake for an additional 15 minutes until the top is puffed and golden.

While the pudding is baking, make the caramel: Poke a few holes in the top of the can of sweetened condensed milk. Set the can in a saucepan and add water to reach about three-quarters of the way up the can. Bring the water to a rolling boil and cook for 25 minutes, adding more water if it reduces too much. Remove the can from the water and allow to cool for a few minutes before opening.

Serve the bread pudding warm, drizzled with milk caramel and garnished with whipped cream and Heath bits.

THE FORK & WRENCH

2322 BOSTON STREET
BALTIMORE, MD 21224
(443) 759-9360
THEFORKANDWRENCH.COM
OWNERS: ANDY GRUVER, JASON SANCHEZ
CHEF: CYRUS KEEFER

When the old Pur Lounge space was being refurbished, all people could talk about was what that interior would look like when it was done. Andy Gruver and Jason Sanchez worked for two years to create a visually interesting space in what was to become their restaurant, the Fork & Wrench. They created a series of quirky dining rooms over three floors and a courtyard, and the decor includes salvaged materials from an old bank building, a former mental institution, and a factory. There are framed insect collections on the walls, shelves of old books, and even new wallpaper made to look old by being hung, distressed, then pulled down in strips. The restaurant is so full of things to look at, some diners take a little tour of the place before settling down with a menu.

The chef at the Fork & Wrench is Cyrus Keefer, most recently at Birroteca and who before that ran the kitchen at several notable Rehoboth Beach restaurants. Keefer has cooked at the James Beard House in New York, participating with other Baltimore-area chefs including the Food Market's Chad Gauss in a five-course dinner that celebrated the cuisine of the Chesapeake Bay region. He also won the People's Choice award for his blue-crab-and-white-corn raviolini at the 2011 Crab Bash, an event held at the B&O Brasserie every September.

Keefer keeps the menu at the Fork & Wrench fairly short, with a handful of appetizer-y first and second courses, and nine or ten entrees. The menu changes weekly and is dependent on what's available at the farmers' markets around town. Keefer believes in buying "pristine ingredients and having a great relationship with local farmers, seamen, and other producers." He's proud to see that this is the way the tide has turned, and that many modern restaurants are feeling the same way.

"The dining scene in Baltimore is growing, and I think diners have really opened up to creative foods and are more willing to try new things." The oil-poached calamari and short rib tortelli are the big sellers on the Fork & Wrench menu, but the chef isn't afraid to try out innovative combinations like grilled octopus paired with lamb meatballs or braised veal cheeks and lobster.

Escargot Buns

(SERVES 8)

For the escargots:

1 can helix escargots
1 tablespoon minced shallots
1 clove garlic, minced
1 fresh bay leaf
2 tablespoons minced carrot
1 tablespoon salt
1 star anise
4 cups chicken stock

For the garlic butter:

1 pound unsalted butter (divided)
4 tablespoons minced garlic
2 tablespoons minced shallot
1 bay leaf
1 tablespoon white soy sauce
1 tablespoon sea salt

For the buns:

1 tablespoon fresh yeast
1 tablespoon sugar
6 cups plus 1 tablespoon high-gluten flour,
    preferably King Arthur
1 tablespoon salt
1 tablespoon olive oil

For serving:

Sea salt
Leftover garlic butter
Finely chopped scallions and chives
Reserved escargot poaching liquid

To make the escargots: Drain the escargots from their brine and rinse very well.

Place all ingredients in a saucepan with the escargots and simmer for 45 minutes. Allow the snails to cool in the cooking liquid, then strain, reserving the liquid.

To make the garlic butter: Melt ½ pound of the butter and add the remaining ingredients. Cook for about 20 minutes, until the garlic and shallots are translucent. Allow the butter to cool slightly and whip in the other ½ pound of butter. Once incorporated, refrigerate until ready to use.

To make the buns: Place the yeast, sugar, 1 tablespoon of flour, and 1 tablespoon of warm water in the bowl of a stand mixer with a dough hook. Allow this starter to bloom, about 25 minutes or until bubbling.

Add the remaining 6 cups of flour and the salt to the starter. Turn the mixer on low power and gradually add about 1½ cups of warm water until a dough forms. The dough should be a bit sticky. Turn up the power to medium-high speed and continue mixing until the dough forms a ball and no longer sticks to the sides of the bowl, about 8 minutes.

Turn the dough out onto a floured surface. Cover and let rise for 45 minutes or until double in size.

Once the dough has risen, punch it down. Cut 2-ounce portions from the dough, roll each piece into a ball, and then flatten each ball into a disk.

Place three snails in the center of each dough disk and top with one teaspoon of the garlic butter. Pull the ends of the dough up around the snails and pinch the top closed. Roll the ball between your palms to create a smooth ball.

Cook the balls by baking in a preheated 500°F oven, or steam them for about 8 minutes, as they do at the restaurant. (You can purchase steamer baskets at any kitchen store; follow manufacturer's instructions.) When steamed balls are done, pan fry them until crisp in a little oil.

To serve: Sprinkle the buns with a bit of sea salt and top them with more garlic butter, fresh scallions, and chives. Serve with the reserved poaching broth for dunking.

Gertrude's

BALTIMORE MUSEUM OF ART
10 ART MUSEUM DRIVE
BALTIMORE, MD 21218
(410) 889-3399
JOHNSHIELDS.COM/RESTAURANT/REST/GERTRUDES.HTML
OWNER: CHEF JOHN SHIELDS

After spending years cooking in coastal spots around the country like Cape Cod and San Francisco, Baltimore native John Shields came home and put some serious thought into the particular coastal cuisine of the Chesapeake Bay. This spurred the PBS cooking shows and their companion cookbooks *Chesapeake Bay Cooking* and *Coastal Cooking,* which celebrate the bounty of seafood available on the East Coast and in Maryland in particular.

He opened his restaurant, Gertrude's, in 1998, in a plum spot at the Baltimore Museum of Art, next to the Johns Hopkins University Homewood campus. It took time for the restaurant to establish itself as an entity separate from the museum, even as it looks over the Sculpture Garden and its collection of works by artists like Calder and Rodin. A seat on the terrace is a lovely place to enjoy Chef Shields's cuisine, but so is the sophisticated dining room, the decor of which is inspired by life on the Eastern Shore.

The menu is all about Chesapeake cuisine, as befits a restaurant owned by the man who literally wrote the book on the subject. There are oysters and crab soup, and crab

cakes, of course, made from a recipe by John Shields's beloved grandmother Gertrude. Shields understands that diners "tend to like something familiar, but with a twist," so he uses a saffron mayo in his crab imperial and heaps it into a portobello mushroom. Despite the plethora of seafood on the menu, Gertrude's is also the perfect restaurant for those who are squeamish about crustaceans and mollusks. The chef himself prefers to eat a mostly meat-free diet, so you'll also find things like a chickpea-quinoa salad sneaking its way onto the specials menu, as well as the popular I Can't Believe It's Not Crab cakes, made with zucchini.

"Chesapeake cuisine is all about taking the freshest and brightest of what is available and doing very little to it." While the whole farm-to-table movement has become a guiding force for many new restaurants, Shields notes that it was the way man ate for thousands of years. And hopefully will be for many years to come.

Crispy Rockfish Tacos
with Lime Jicama Slaw & Avocado Cream
(SERVES 4)

For the lime jicama slaw:

1 cup shredded cabbage
½ cup shredded jicama
¼ cup chopped green onion
¼ cup julienned carrots
1 tablespoon chopped cilantro
Juice of 1 lime
¼ cup mayonnaise

For the avocado cream:

2 ripe avocados, peeled and pit removed
½ cup sour cream
Juice of ½ lime
Pinch of ground cumin
Salt, to taste

For the salsa fresca:

3 large ripe tomatoes, cored, seeded, and diced
½ red onion, finely diced

1 serrano chile, seeded and minced
1 jalapeño chile, seeded and minced
Juice of 1 lime, or more to taste
1 teaspoon salt
¼ cup finely chopped cilantro

For the tacos:

1 pound rockfish fillets
1 cup flour
2 teaspoons salt
1 teaspoon cumin
1 teaspoon garlic powder
½ teaspoon chipotle powder
½ teaspoon paprika
¼ teaspoon cayenne pepper
¼ teaspoon freshly ground black pepper
Oil for frying
16 fresh corn tortillas
Sliced radishes
Lime wedges

To make the lime jicama slaw: Mix all ingredients together in a bowl. Cover and refrigerate for 1 hour before serving.

To make the avocado cream: Place the avocados in a bowl and mash well. Stir in the remaining ingredients and mix well. Cover and refrigerate until ready to use.

To make the salsa fresca: Mix all ingredients together in a bowl.

To make the tacos: Cut the rockfish fillets into 1½-inch chunks. In a bowl mix the flour and seasonings and blend well. Add about 1½ inches of cooking oil to a large heavy pot and heat until quite hot, about 350°F. Dust the rockfish pieces in the flour and shake off the excess. In batches, fry the fish until golden brown and cooked through. Remove the pieces of fish with a slotted utensil and allow to drain on paper towels. Keep warm.

While cooking the fish, heat a dry (not oiled) cast-iron skillet and warm the tortillas for about 30 seconds on each side. Wrap the warmed tortillas in a damp towel while heating the rest.

To assemble the tacos: Place a spoonful of slaw in the center of each tortilla, followed by several pieces of fish, and a dollop of avocado cream. Garnish with a teaspoon of salsa and slices of radish. Serve lime wedges on the side.

LUMP CRAB & ROASTED CORN BRUSCHETTA

(SERVES 6–8)

1½ pounds ripe plum tomatoes, peeled, seeded, and diced

2 teaspoons minced garlic

2 tablespoons extra virgin olive oil

¼ cup finely chopped fresh basil

1 teaspoon balsamic vinegar

⅓ cup finely diced fresh mozzarella (optional)

Kernels cut from 2–3 ears roasted or charred corn (see Note)

Salt and freshly ground black pepper, to taste

½ pound lump crabmeat, picked over for shells

1 baguette

¼ cup olive oil for brushing

Note: To roast corn, preheat oven to 400°F. Place the ears, still in their husks, directly on the oven rack. Roast for about 20–25 minutes. Remove from the oven and allow to cool slightly. Husk the corn and, when ready to use, cut the kernels from the cob.

To char corn, husk the ears and place them over a medium gas flame on a stovetop burner. With tongs, keep turning the corn, allowing it to just barely blacken in spots around the cob, about 5 minutes' cooking time. Cut the kernels from the cob.

In a mixing bowl combine the tomatoes, garlic, olive oil, basil, and vinegar. Fold in the mozzarella, if using, and the kernels of roasted corn. Season the mixture with salt and pepper to taste. Carefully fold in the crabmeat, taking care not to break up the lumps.

Preheat oven to 425°F.

Slice the baguette on a diagonal, about ½ inch thick. Lightly brush each side of the baguette pieces with olive oil. Place bread pieces on a sheet tray and bake for about 2–3 minutes, or until they are just lightly browned.

Place the toasted bread on a serving tray and top each piece with a heaping tablespoon or so of the tomato-corn-crab mixture. Serve at once.

Grano Emporio

1031 W 36th Street
Baltimore, MD 21211
(443) 869-3429
GRANOPASTABAR.COM/EMPORIO
Owner: Chef Gino Troia

Gino Troia has many talents. After his family emigrated from Naples in the 1960s, he enrolled at the Maryland Institute College of Art to study interior design. Some years later he traded his measuring tape for scissors and opened Troia Hair Studio in Towson. Eventually he and his brother Ernesto, a chef at Little Italy's Vellegia's, opened Troia Brothers' International Market and Café, which in 1988 became a full-fledged restaurant that they called Café Troia. After nearly a decade at the family restaurant, Gino went off on his own to start restaurants at the Walters Art Museum and in Canton before opening a tiny pasta bar in Hampden—Grano.

Grano's concept was simple: offer a selection of sauces and a selection of pastas and let the customer choose his or her own custom dish. Since there was no room for storage, everything was made fresh daily. There weren't even any tables at first, but when people decided to stick around to eat their food, Gino had to put in a few to supplement the stools at the counter. The overwhelming success of Grano Pasta Bar led to the establishment of a more traditional restaurant down the street called Grano Emporio.

Combining traditional Italian cuisine with a modern focus on local and seasonal ingredients, Grano Emporio's menu is lighter than what many might think of as Italian

food. While there's still plenty of pasta, particular emphasis is placed on seafood, and sauces are more likely to involve olive oil and pesto than tomatoes. The menu offerings are complemented by a selection of Italian wines and beer.

Not only a chef and restaurateur, Gino Troia is a food historian and a certified sommelier. And in his spare time (what spare time?) he graciously acts as a tour guide. In the summer and fall, Troia offers culinary guided tours of his homeland that include cooking demonstrations and visits to wine producers. The tours are meant for those who wish to escape their busy lifestyles and immerse themselves in the simple pleasures of new food and new people.

Caponata

(SERVES 5)

You can serve this wonderful Sicilian dish on a toasted country bread, bruschetta style, as a complement to fish or white meats, or even tossed with your favorite pasta.

3 Italian eggplants, diced

Coarse salt

1 large red or yellow bell pepper

3 tablespoons extra virgin olive oil (divided)

1 red onion, diced

4 celery stalks, diced

2 tablespoons salt-packed capers, rinsed

6 large, ripe local tomatoes, diced

4 cloves fresh garlic, smashed with a large knife

2 tablespoons red wine vinegar

Pinch of brown sugar

Pinch of crushed red pepper

Sea salt

3 tablespoons fresh basil leaves, torn by hand

Sprinkle the eggplant pieces with coarse salt and allow to rest for 30–45 minutes. Drain in a colander, then blot dry.

Roast the bell pepper under the broiler or over a gas flame until charred. Place in a paper bag or in a bowl covered with plastic wrap until cool enough to handle. When cool, remove the skin and seeds under running water, then cut the pepper into half-inch squares.

Heat 2 tablespoons of the olive oil in a large sauté pan. Cook the onion until translucent. Add the celery, stirring frequently, and cook an additional few minutes until the vegetables start to brown. Add the capers, tomatoes, and bell pepper and stir to combine.

In a separate pan, heat 1 tablespoon of olive oil and add the eggplant. Stir to coat, then add the garlic cloves. Cook until lightly browned, then transfer the eggplant and garlic to the pan with the rest of the vegetables.

Add the vinegar, sugar, and crushed red pepper and stir to combine. Add sea salt to taste. Garnish with the torn basil.

Gypsy Queen Food Truck

GYPSYQUEENCAFE.COM
OWNERS: TOM LOONEY, ED SCHERER, CHEF ANNMARIE LANGTON

In 2010, after fifteen years of running the popular Canton restaurant Helen's Garden, owners Tom Looney and Ed Scherer decided to call it quits. It didn't take long, however, for the two of them, along with Helen's Garden's executive chef Annmarie Langton, to start another business, this time taking it to the streets—literally—in the form of the Gypsy Queen Café.

The Gypsy Queen trucks might possibly be the most popular food trucks in Baltimore. Scratch that—they *are* the most popular food trucks in Baltimore. Not only have they received accolades from the *City Paper* and *Baltimore* magazine for three years running, they also smashed the competition in the last two battles between Baltimore and Washington, DC, food trucks known as the Taste of Two Cities. There are two Gypsy Queens so far, but Chef Langton says, "Our goal is to have five trucks on the road. We're having fun!"

They're definitely having a good time—just look at the menu. The Gypsy Queen's most popular item is something called the Crab Cone. Now wrap your mind around this: a large waffle cone (yes, an ice cream cone) filled with french fries, topped with lump

crab cakes, and doused with a spicy chipotle mayonnaise. In the cooler months, they also sell a version filled with macaroni and cheese. Yes, both versions come with forks, which make the cones eminently portable lunches.

But that's not all by a long shot. Those tasty crab cakes come in taco form (our favorite), as do myriad other types of protein. We've even happily been guinea pigs for a beet-beef-and-feta taco that was amazing. There are pork banh mi sandwiches, cheesesteaks of various ethnic origins that would make even the strictest Philadelphian a believer, and a fried fish sandwich served with American cheese on Texas toast that can turn any day of the week into Friday.

In addition to being found all over town during workday lunchtimes, the Gypsy Queens join Baltimore's other food trucks at the almost-weekly al fresco dining events called the Gathering. "The Gatherings are a good thing," says Langton. "They bring a lot of people together to eat good street food, listen to good music, and just let loose. It's a mobile festival!" They're held on Fridays for much of the year, but the location varies, so make sure to check out thegatheringbaltimore.com for more information.

CHIPOTLE AIOLI

(MAKES 1 CUP)

While this sauce is a component of the taco, we believe it deserves to be listed as a standalone recipe because it's so simple and so good. We like to put it in everything, from egg salad to hamburgers.

1 cup mayonnaise
1 garlic clove, chopped
2 teaspoons chipotle in adobo
½ bunch fresh cilantro
2 teaspoons sugar

Combine all ingredients in a food processor or mix well by hand until the sugar is dissolved.

GYPSY QUEEN'S SOFT-SHELL CRAB BLT
(SERVES 1)

The Gypsy Queen folks deep-fry their soft-shells, but you can cook them in a sauté pan with a couple tablespoons of oil if you have a Fear of Frying.

6 cups vegetable oil

2 cups flour

1 tablespoon Old Bay seasoning

½ tablespoon ground pepper

2 eggs

For each sandwich:

1 medium-size soft-shell crab, cleaned
(face and gills removed)

2 slices Texas toast

⅓ cup thinly shredded cabbage

1 tablespoon chipotle aioli (recipe on p. 57)

2 slices fresh local tomatoes

2 slices applewood smoked bacon, cooked crisp

Place the oil in a deep, heavy, medium-sized pot or deep fryer and heat to 350°F.

Combine the flour, Old Bay, and pepper in a bowl. In a separate bowl, whisk together the eggs and ¼ cup of water.

Coat each crab with the seasoned flour, then dip it into the egg wash. Give it another coat of the seasoned flour and gently shake off the excess.

Carefully lower the crab into the hot oil using a pair of tongs. Cook for approximately 2 minutes on each side, until golden brown. Remove from the oil with the tongs and place on a paper-towel-lined plate.

For each sandwich, toast two slices of Texas toast. Top one slice with cabbage, ½ tablespoon of aioli, tomatoes, bacon, and then the fried crab. Top with another ½ tablespoon of the aioli and the remaining slice of toast.

THE FARMS IN FARM-TO-TABLE

Mingodale Farm

The Hereford-Parkton area of Maryland has a long history of family farming, and Mingodale Farm (mingo dalefarm.com) has been around since 1760. The Foster family has run the farm for generations, providing a wide range of produce including berries, corn, squash, potatoes, and herbs. They are particularly proud of their asparagus, tomatoes, garlic, and gourmet peppers. The dairy barn was converted into a henhouse where the free-range birds provide loads of fresh eggs. Visitors can pick their own produce during the summer, or seek out a special Halloween pumpkin in the fall.

Heavy Seas Alehouse

1300 Bank Street
Baltimore, MD 21231
(410) 522-0850
HEAVYSEASALEHOUSE.COM
OWNERS: PATRICK DAHLGREN, VINCE CASSINO
CHEF: MATT SEEBER

Heavy Seas Alehouse has its roots in Sisson's, a Federal Hill tavern opened in 1980. In 1989, after a law was passed allowing Maryland bars to brew their own beer, Sisson's became Maryland's first brewpub. A few years later, owner Hugh Sisson realized he was more interested in the brewing side of the business and went off to concentrate on beer making. The eventual result was Heavy Seas, one of Baltimore's best-known craft breweries.

Sisson's former GM Vince Cassino and Hugh's stepson Patrick Dahlgren own the brewery's namesake Alehouse. It's located in the old Holland Tack Factory building, where one is now far more likely to find burgers and fries than the tacks, brads, and nails once churned out for use in everything from bulletin boards to major league baseballs. The restaurant naturally features Heavy Seas beers and has adopted the brewery's skull-and-crossbones pirate logo as its own.

They like to say that the Heavy Seas Alehouse is "Where Great Beer Meets Great Food," and to drive that point home, the Alehouse's kitchen is run by Matt Seeber, veteran of many a fine restaurant, including Aureole, Tabla, and Gramercy Tavern in New York. Most notably, Seeber was executive chef at Tom Colicchio's Vegas restaurant Craftsteak, and he is proud to call Colicchio both a mentor and a friend. Seeber brings his fine dining chops to the Alehouse, insisting on cooking everything to order and using the freshest ingredients—locally sourced if possible. While the beer-friendly food seems fairly simple, there are subtly elegant touches, like the perfect 63°C poached farm egg atop a salad of chicory with bacon, or the saffron-enhanced mayo that accompanies an order of onion rings in a Loose Cannon beer batter.

"We like to call it 'approachable restaurant food,'" says Seeber. "Here at Heavy Seas Alehouse, we put as much sophistication and attention to detail into our preparation and presentation as some of the more notoriously high-end restaurants I have worked in, like Gramercy Tavern. Truthfully, it's the only way I know how to cook. Customers get the benefit of high-quality food at a much more reasonable price.

"Most of our patrons are truly engaged in both our process and our food. They have realized that we are doing things a little differently than other restaurants in the area. Baltimore's food scene is becoming stronger and more sophisticated every day and we are trying to play a role in that. I am pushing the boundaries with what people expect at an alehouse or pub, but still remaining familiar to both Heavy Seas and Baltimore. Of course, we also have patrons who are just looking for great food and we certainly deliver that at Heavy Seas Alehouse, as well."

Chicory Salad with a Poached Egg

(SERVES 4)

If you happen to have one of those fancy home *sous vide* gadgets, like the SousVide Supreme, cook your eggs—in their shells—at 63°C (145.4°F) for 45 minutes. Crack the eggs onto a paper towel to catch any excess moisture before placing them on your salad.

4 ounces thick-cut bacon
2 tablespoons white vinegar
4 eggs
1 teaspoon champagne vinegar
1 tablespoon whole grain mustard

2 heads frisée or other chicory greens, trimmed and washed
4 tablespoons blue cheese crumbles
2 tablespoons thinly sliced scallion greens
Sea salt and freshly cracked black pepper
Parmesan cheese

Cut the bacon into strips (lardons). Cook until crisp. Remove the lardons to a plate and reserve the rendered bacon fat.

Break each egg into a small ramekin. Bring a pot of water to a boil and add the white vinegar. Reduce the heat to just above a simmer and gently lower the eggs into the water. Poach gently for about 4 minutes, or until desired doneness.

In a large bowl, combine the champagne vinegar, mustard, and reserved bacon fat. Add the greens, blue cheese, scallions, and bacon, tossing to coat.

Arrange the salad on four plates, making sure everything is evenly distributed. Make a small well in each salad and place a poached egg in it. Season the egg with sea salt and cracked black pepper. Sprinkle with freshly grated Parmesan cheese and serve.

J. Paul's

301 Light Street
Baltimore, MD 21202
(410) 659-1889
J-PAULS.CAPITALRESTAURANTS.COM
Owner: Capital Restaurant Concepts
Chef: Jason Dyke

Baltimore's Inner Harbor, home to the National Aquarium and the Maryland Science Center, has long been a popular area for visitors and locals alike. On a sunny day, one of those perfect days when the sky is blue and the seagulls are chattering, the Promenade is usually bustling with pedestrians taking in the sights, visiting the attractions, or just hanging out. And there's no better place for people-watching than the patio at J. Paul's in Harborplace's Light Street Pavilion.

Whether you want to slurp down a dozen (or more) oysters or settle down to a multicourse meal, J. Paul's can satisfy your urge. The restaurant, which has been at Harborplace for over fifteen years now, straddles the line between casual and elegant dining in order to appeal to the broad range of patrons—both tourists and locals—that the waterside location tends to attract.

The man in charge of the kitchen at J. Paul's is Chef Jason Dyke, who was born and raised in the Baltimore area and has worked all over the country. He's happy to see that the Baltimore dining scene, while not on the same scale as New York or Chicago, is "definitely carving a niche in the Mid-Atlantic region." His personal preference is for

"clean, quality product, properly seasoned, prepared with proper cooking techniques," and he gets to exercise that preference in everything from the perfect mignonette that is served with your choice of oysters to dishes like his crab cake appetizer, which was a big hit with us on a visit to J. Paul's last summer. We also enjoy Dyke's crab soup, which has a tomato-and-seafood-based broth and is a bit different from the traditional soups made with meat stock.

J. Paul's also serves brunch on the weekends, and the Hangover Hash is as sure a cure for that ailment as any we've tried.

HANGOVER HASH

(SERVES 2)

For the caramelized onions:

2 tablespoons olive oil
2 cups sliced onions
Pinch of salt

For the hash:

4 cups diced potatoes
1 tablespoon oil
½ cup diced bell peppers
½ cup diced white onions
½ cup andouille sausage, roughly chopped
2 teaspoons chopped garlic
4 ounces heavy cream
4 tablespoons chopped fresh herbs (parsley, oregano, tarragon—whatever you like)
Salt and pepper, to taste
1–2 tablespoons butter
4 eggs

For assembly:

2 slices sourdough bread
Melted butter

To make the onions: Heat the olive oil in a medium skillet over high heat. Add the onions and a generous pinch of salt.

Cook, stirring frequently, until the onion starts to brown, about 5 minutes. Reduce heat and add a tablespoon or so of water. Cover the pan and continue to cook for an additional 15 minutes, stirring occasionally. When the onion is very tender and golden brown, remove from heat.

To make the hash: Blanch the potatoes in boiling salted water for about 3 minutes. Drain well and set aside.

Heat oil in a sauté pan over medium heat. Cook potatoes, bell peppers, onions, andouille sausage, and garlic until vegetables are tender. Add the heavy cream and half of the herbs and cook until the cream has been absorbed. Add salt and pepper to taste.

Coat a nonstick pan with the butter. Over medium heat, cook the eggs sunny-side up.

To serve: Toast the bread and butter it. Place the potato-pepper mixture in two serving dishes and top each with two eggs, caramelized onion, and the remainder of the chopped herbs. Serve with the buttered toast.

MARYLAND CRAB SOUP

(SERVES 12–15)

Maryland crab soup can be made with any of several base flavors, beef and ham being among the most popular. Chef Dyke's version is based on tomato and crab stock, resulting in a more delicate flavor that doesn't compete with the crab itself.

1 yellow onion, diced
½ head celery, diced
2 carrots, diced
1 tablespoon chopped garlic
3 Idaho potatoes, diced
2 cups corn kernels
1 tablespoon Old Bay seasoning
1 tablespoon dried basil
2 tablespoons Worcestershire sauce
½ tablespoon Tabasco sauce
1 quart tomato juice
½ cup tomato paste

2 quarts crab stock
1 pound jumbo lump crabmeat

In a stockpot, sauté the onion, celery, carrot, and garlic until tender. Add all remaining ingredients except the crabmeat, stir well, and simmer for 1 hour.

Remove from heat, cool, and refrigerate.

To serve, reheat the soup. Ladle into bowls, adding a mound of fresh crabmeat to each bowl.

JACK'S BISTRO

3123 ELLIOTT STREET
BALTIMORE, MD 21224
(410) 878-6542
JACKSBISTRO.NET
OWNERS: CHEF TED STELZENMULLER, MICHELE JACKSON

One might call Jack's Bistro funky, but "eclectic" might be a more accurate word. The rowhouse restaurant in Baltimore's Canton neighborhood is named after Jack Tripper's place on the '70s sitcom *Three's Company,* but Jack's is no fern bar. Owner-Chef Ted Stelzenmuller and his wife and general manager Christie Smertycha have put together a friendly neighborhood joint with a great bar and a kitchen that fuses modernist techniques and international flavors with classics like filet mignon and crab cakes.

A fervent world traveler, Stelzenmuller often whips up specials based on the location most recently visited, be it Singapore or Morocco. "We close the restaurant twice a year to travel to a distant land and bring back the best that region has to offer. In the past five years, I have been to over a dozen and a half nations on five continents. The diversity of Jack's Bistro's menu is a reflection of all our travels, both foreign and domestic. I have found who I am as a cook as a result of this, and I am always eager to plan for the next culinary getaway."

Jack's was the first restaurant to introduce the technique of cooking *sous vide* to Baltimore. Food, proteins especially, are vacuum-sealed in plastic pouches (the term literally means "under vacuum") and cooked in a water bath that holds a precise temperature, often for days at a time. At Jack's one can find duck and Wagyu sirloin steak cooked *sous vide.* And don't dare ask for that sirloin to be cooked above medium-rare, because the 134°F temperature is absolutely perfect and creates a wonderful silky texture in the meat. As for the dishes with a strong international flair, among them a Malaysian Laksa and an Indian curry made with green lentils, Chef Ted often spends years practicing specific cooking techniques just to get it right. "I love everything about food," he says, even the hard work.

There's also the occasional quirky dish that ends up being a best seller, like the Mac + Cheese + Chocolate. It's exactly what it sounds like—macaroni and cheese made with shell-

shaped pasta in a smoky cheese sauce, topped with dark chocolate shavings. And if that's not quirky enough, how about Logom, the Swedish snack that wraps a hot dog, shrimp salad, and mashed potatoes in a flatbread. "We have some of the best patrons here at Jack's. They are always eager to try all of the adventurous dishes that I bring back from my travels. I will never forget the first time I put the Singapore classic Pig's Organ Soup on the menu. It was so well received that I have not held anything back since then."

When approached to contribute to this book, Ted was enthusiastic. "I believe those cooking at home are more skilled than ever. Cooking has become 'cool' again, and I couldn't be more excited about that."

We couldn't agree more.

CUCUMBER & TOMATO CAESAR SALAD WITH FETA CROUTONS
(SERVES 2)

For the feta croutons:

¼ cup feta cheese cut into ½-inch cubes
⅓ cup cornstarch
Oil for frying

For the dressing:

1 egg yolk
1 teaspoon capers
1 teaspoon chopped fresh parsley
2 teaspoons fresh lemon juice
3 anchovies (optional)
1 tablespoon freshly grated Parmesan cheese
½ teaspoon chopped garlic
3 drops Worcestershire sauce
1 drop Tabasco
Pinch of black pepper
1 tablespoon Dijon mustard
1¼ cups canola oil

For assembly:

1 cucumber, peeled
1 heirloom tomato

To make the feta croutons: Roll the feta cubes in the cornstarch to coat. Shake off the excess. Heat a few tablespoons of oil in a skillet over medium-high heat. Fry the feta for a minute or so, turning the cubes to brown all sides.

To make the dressing: Place all dressing ingredients except for the oil in a blender. Turn the blender on and add the oil in a slow stream. Blend until emulsified. The dressing should be mayonnaise-like in consistency.

To assemble: Slice the cucumber thinly lengthwise on a mandoline slicer. Cut the tomato in wedges. Toss the cucumber and tomato with dressing to taste. Arrange the vegetables on a plate, layering the cucumber ribbons and tomato wedges to add height. Top with feta croutons.

LANGERMANN'S

2400 BOSTON STREET, #101A
BALTIMORE, MD 21224
(410) 534-3287
LANGERMANNS.COM
OWNERS: CHEF NEAL LANGERMANN, DAVID MCGILL, MARK LASKER,
JIMI CHUNG

During the seventeenth century, the coastal area along South Carolina was a major shipping port. The cultures of Africa, France, Portugal, Spain, and the native Powhatan Indians came together, and the disparate mix of cuisines, coupled with the plentiful seafood available, formed what is now known as "lowcountry" cuisine. This is the basis of the menu at Neal Langermann's eponymous restaurant.

Chef Langermann says that lowcountry cuisine is "more of a celebration of life and food than of any particular dish or ingredients. From a historical perspective, there is either the magnificent showy home in town or the simple plantation house on the river. Traditionally there has been little to no middle ground. You either dined in Georgian grandeur or you peeled your own shrimp. You entertained or you served. It is this balance of high and low that distinguishes the lowcountry."

Prior to opening his own restaurant, Neal Langermann made a name for himself in the DC culinary scene, where he cooked at Red Sage and Georgia Brown's and was

named Chef of the Year by the Restaurant Association of Metropolitan Washington in 2001. Then he moved to Baltimore, a city he felt was on the cusp of a culinary revival. "The city was on the verge of shedding its reputation and attracting some serious culinary talent," says the chef, who decided he wanted to be a part of the new scene.

Today Langermann's has two outposts, in Canton and Federal Hill. Both restaurants offer a casual and comfortable ambience and the fine cuisine of a chef who takes tremendous care to showcase the best of southern cooking. Among the best-selling dishes at Langermann's are the Cape Fear scallops and the tuna crab tartare, the recipes for which can be found in *Food Lovers' Guide to Baltimore* (Globe Pequot Press). Langermann believes they're popular because "the flavors are layered in such a way that one needs to actually slow down and think about what they are eating. Too much of our food these days is consumed while distracted. I feel these dishes win people over because they make you think and contribute to your own pleasure. Each bite is somewhat different and somewhat the same. It invites conversation, sharing, and involvement."

Roast Tenderloin of Beef au Poivre with Potato Gratin

(SERVES 10–12)

"Every day we bring in fresh seasonal ingredients and, using classic French cooking techniques, create dishes that express old favorites in new ways. Such is the case with my Roast Tenderloin of Beef au Poivre. The secret to this dish is patience. The whole process takes a good hour, but by slowly bringing the meat to the desired temperature, in this case medium rare, the meat will be amazingly tender."

For the espresso rub:

6 tablespoons ground black pepper
6 tablespoons kosher salt
2 tablespoons paprika
2 tablespoons onion powder
6 tablespoons espresso powder
1 tablespoon cayenne
½ cup sugar

For the white cheddar potato gratin:

1 quart heavy cream
½ pound shredded Parmesan cheese
½ pound shredded white cheddar cheese
2 tablespoons salt and pepper mix
1 teaspoon ground nutmeg
4 pounds thinly sliced Idaho potatoes

For the Madagascar green peppercorn sauce:

2 ounces thinly sliced shallots
1 ounce butter
2 tablespoons green peppercorns in brine, drained
1 quart demiglace
Salt and pepper, to taste

For the beef:

1 tenderloin of beef, about 5–6 pounds, cleaned
3 ounces olive oil
½ cup espresso rub
½ cup brown sugar
½ cup chopped herbs, preferably parsley and thyme

To make the espresso rub: Combine all ingredients in a bowl.

To make the white cheddar potato gratin: Preheat oven to 350°F.

In a large bowl, combine the cream, cheeses, and seasonings, making sure everything is evenly distributed. Pour half the mixture into another bowl and add the potato slices to the first bowl.

Layer the potato slices in a 9 x 13 x 2-inch baking pan. Press down on the potatoes to ensure a tight, even fit. Pour the remaining liquid over the potatoes. Cover the pan with foil and bake for 1 hour. Remove the foil and allow the potatoes to brown for an additional 15 minutes. The gratin is done when a toothpick inserted into the center comes out clean.

To make the Madagascar green peppercorn sauce: In a small saucepan, sauté the shallots in butter until translucent. Add the peppercorns and demiglace and allow to simmer for 15 minutes. Adjust for seasoning and continue to cook until the sauce coats the back of a spoon.

To make the beef: On a clean surface rub the beef tenderloin with 1 ounce of the olive oil until evenly coated. Combine the espresso rub and brown sugar in a bowl. Add the chopped herbs and mix thoroughly. Coat the tenderloin on all sides. Refrigerate for 2 hours.

Preheat oven to 400°F.

In a large sauté pan, heat the remaining 2 ounces of olive oil and sear the beef tenderloin on all sides until nicely browned. Place on a sheet pan and set in the oven.

Cook the beef until the internal temperature reaches 100°F. Remove from the oven and allow to rest for 15 minutes. Return the beef to the oven and cook to an internal temperature of 110°F. Remove from the oven and let rest 15 minutes. Return the beef to the oven and cook to an internal temperature of 120°F. Remove from the oven and allow to rest for an additional 15 minutes.

When ready to eat, return the beef to the oven for the final time and cook until the internal temperature reaches 125–130°F. Remove to a cutting board. Allow to rest for 8 minutes.

Slice the meat. Serve over white cheddar potato gratin and top with Madagascar green peppercorn sauce.

FARMS IN FARM-TO-TABLE

Roseda Black Angus Farm

The beef industry has come under a great deal of scrutiny in recent years since the emphasis on mass production has created less than flavorful results. Ed Burchell, owner of Roseda Beef (rosedabeef.com), feels that merging the best of old-fashioned breeding techniques with modern technology can produce healthier cattle and tastier beef. Instead of using hormones or antibiotics, Roseda cattle are fed a natural diet including corn, hay, grass, alfalfa, and soybean meal, plus vitamins and minerals. The beef is also dry-aged for 14 to 21 days to ensure great flavor and tenderness. Using special tracking software, every cut of Roseda Beef can be traced back to the specific animal. And if you think you can get Roseda Beef only in fine dining establishments, Orioles great Cal Ripkin Jr. offers a line of frozen hamburgers made with 100 percent Roseda Black Angus Beef that can be purchased at many local supermarkets.

Liv2Eat

1444 Light Street
Baltimore, MD 21230
(443) 449-7129
liv2eat.com
Owners: Chef Kevin Perry, Cecilia Benalcazar

"People eat to live. We live to eat." This sentiment is a truism for those of us who love food; it also inspired the name of a relative newcomer to the Federal Hill restaurant scene. Opened in November of 2012, Liv2Eat has garnered high praise from local foodies and restaurant critics and even snagged the *City Paper*'s Best New Restaurant award for 2013. The paper raves about everything from the restaurant's comfortable ambience to the service to—of course—the seasonally inspired eats.

The man responsible for the food at Liv2Eat is Chef Kevin Perry, who previously worked at Equinox in DC and Hell's Point Seafood in Annapolis. He and his wife, Cecilia Benalcazar, who has twenty years of business experience, felt that with their combined love of food, culture, and wine, they were up to the challenge of opening their own restaurant. Benalcazar likes to joke that they "thrive on stress." The couple found a storefront in Federal Hill that had good bones (and had been home to more than one restaurant in the recent past) and gave the space some much-needed TLC including

fresh paint and fixtures. The restaurant seats 70, with an additional 25 seats in the lovely back courtyard area.

The menu at Liv2Eat is short and sweet, with a handful of starters, mains, and salads. Perry changes his offerings with the season, but best-selling dishes like the risotto fritters and the various seasonal preparations of Amish chicken are available year-round. Perry doesn't like to overthink things. "My culinary philosophy is, keep it simple. Use fresh local ingredients. Don't cut corners. Be true to fundamental cooking—no need to invent food. Work on your knife skills and always learn whenever you can." He's also a bit of a poet. When I asked him about his favorite food to cook and eat, he replied, "Pigs, pork, and swine. I eat them all the time; because they're fat, because they're flavorful, because they're fine—and they go great with wine."

Can't argue with that.

BBQ Atlantic Salmon
with Corn Sauté & Corn Coulis

(SERVES 6)

For the corn sauté:

2 tablespoons vegetable oil
½ cup minced shallots
12 ears fresh corn, shucked, kernels cut from cobs,
    cobs reserved
¼ cup fresh lemon juice
¾ cup extra virgin olive oil
1 cup tightly packed fresh basil leaves
½ cup julienned piquillo peppers
Salt and freshly ground black pepper

For the corn coulis:

12 corncobs reserved from corn sauté
1 cup corn kernels reserved from corn sauté
1 cup heavy cream
Salt, to taste

For the salmon:

6 (7-ounce) salmon fillets, skinned
Salt and pepper
Vegetable oil
Your favorite barbecue sauce, store-bought or
    homemade
Minced chives, for garnish

To make the corn sauté: Heat the vegetable oil in a large sauté pan over medium-high heat. Add the shallots and sweat, stirring frequently, until soft and translucent but without browning. Add all but 1 cup of corn kernels and reduce heat to medium; cook until tender. Remove from heat. Transfer to a large mixing bowl.

Whisk together the lemon juice and olive oil in a small bowl, then add to the corn. Cut the basil into a fine chiffonade and add it to the corn along with the piquillo peppers. Season with salt and pepper to taste. Set aside at room temperature while you make the corn coulis.

To make the corn coulis: Grate the corncobs on the large holes of a box grater into a large bowl. Discard the cobs.

Put the reserved 1 cup of corn kernels, grated corn, and cream in a medium saucepan. Bring to a simmer over medium-low heat. Stirring frequently, reduce heat to low and simmer until tender. Puree in a blender until smooth. Season with salt. Keep warm.

To make the salmon: Preheat a gas or charcoal grill at least 10 minutes on high heat.

Season both sides of the salmon fillets with salt and pepper. Coat with vegetable oil and place on the hottest part of the grill at a 45-degree angle for 1–2 minutes without moving. Rotate 90° to create cross-hatching, and cook 1–2 minutes more. Flip the salmon fillets and brush with barbecue sauce. Cook 1 minute more or until medium rare.

To serve: Spoon corn coulis onto each of six plates. Top with room-temperature corn sauté. Finish with a salmon fillet and garnish with chives.

Brussels Sprout Salad

(SERVES 6)

¼ cup Dijon mustard

¼ cup white wine vinegar

¾ cup canola oil

2 pounds brussels sprouts

1 head frisée

1 Granny Smith apple

2 tablespoons minced shallots

¼ cup diced, crisply cooked bacon, preferably thick-cut

¼ cup crushed toasted hazelnuts

1 cup finely grated Pecorino

Salt and pepper, to taste

¼ cup finely minced fresh herbs of your choice: tarragon, chives, parsley

Whisk together the mustard and white wine vinegar. Drizzle in the oil while continuing to whisk until completely emulsified.

Wash and dry the raw brussels sprouts and shave them finely. You should have about 8 cups. Place them in a large bowl.

Remove the dark green parts of the frisée. Wash and dry the leaves and cut them into 1-inch pieces until you have 4 cups. Add them to the shaved brussels sprouts.

Peel, core, and julienne the apple. Add it to the bowl.

Add the rest of the ingredients. Toss with the Dijon vinaigrette.

MISS SHIRLEY'S

513 W COLD SPRING LANE
BALTIMORE, MD 21210
(410) 889-5272
MISSSHIRLEYS.COM
OWNER: CRAZY MAN RESTAURANT GROUP
CHEF: BRIGITTE BLEDSOE

The late Baltimore-born entrepreneur Eddie Dopkin originally bought the site on the north side of West Cold Spring Lane to serve as parking for two of his other restaurants, Loco Hombre and Alonzo's. Instead, he opened a new restaurant that he named for Shirley McDowell, a longtime and beloved employee of the Dopkin family.

Miss Shirley's soon outgrew its modest 44-seat building and moved down the street to its current location, which can accommodate 270 hungry patrons. Serving breakfast, lunch, and brunch, the restaurant proved to be so popular that Dopkin opened two other locations, one at Baltimore's Inner Harbor and another in Annapolis.

The vast menu of fanciful pancakes, omelettes, sandwiches, and salads is courtesy of Miss Shirley's corporate executive chef Brigitte Bledsoe, who started with the restaurant in 2005 after answering an ad seeking the "Best Breakfast Chef in the World." Chef Bledsoe says, "I couldn't resist responding, and since I was on crutches at the time, Eddie [Dopkin] came to my house and I cooked a test run for him in my own kitchen. I

made him my crab Benedict and coconut cream stuffed french toast and other dishes that are still on the menu as house specialties."

Chef Bledsoe has always been fascinated with cooking. She started her restaurant career working as a carryout counter girl at a local seafood restaurant and from there worked her way up the line to her current position as Head Kitchen Poobah at all three Miss Shirley's.

While one might think working for a restaurant that specializes in breakfast dishes would be limiting to a chef, Bledsoe exercises her culinary mussel—we mean muscle— by adding seafood to as many items as she can get away with. "People usually think of breakfast food as simple dishes, so I like the challenge of using things like fresh seafood to make dishes more creative and unexpected." She adds, "I love all local seafood. Fresh crabmeat, oysters, flounder, and more. I also love the produce stands that are out in the summer along the Eastern Shore, with Maryland tomatoes and Silver Queen corn. I love the fresh flavors of the Chesapeake region."

Chef Bledsoe really seems to enjoy her job. Despite the occasion being a ways off yet, she says, "I can't wait until the tenth anniversary menu, where I can showcase some of my favorite Miss Shirley's dishes from over the years!"

Fried Green Tomatoes
with Green Tomato Chowchow
& Lemon Herb Mayo

(SERVES 3–4)

For the green tomato chowchow (makes about 1 quart):

1½ cups apple cider vinegar
½ cup water
¼ cup kosher salt
1¼ cups sugar
2 green tomatoes
½ red bell pepper
½ yellow bell pepper
1 small jalapeño pepper
½ Vidalia onion

For the lemon herb mayo (makes about 1 pint):

1 tablespoon roughly chopped fresh basil
½ cup roughly chopped fresh chives
½ cup roughly chopped fresh parsley
⅛ cup lemon juice
1 cup mayonnaise
½ cup sour cream
1 teaspoon Dijon mustard
¼ teaspoon Tabasco sauce
½ teaspoon kosher salt

For the tomatoes:

3 green tomatoes
¼ cup honey
1 pint buttermilk
2 cups yellow cornmeal
1 cup flour
½ cup sugar
2 tablespoons Cajun seasoning
Canola or vegetable oil for frying

To make the chowchow: Combine the vinegar, water, and salt in a small pot and bring to a boil. Once it has come to a boil, turn the pot off and add the sugar, whisking to dissolve.

Cut the tomatoes, peppers, and onion into large dice. In small batches, pulse the vegetables in a food processor until you have a medium-to-fine chop, according to your personal preference.

Add the vegetable mix to the hot vinegar mixture and stir to incorporate. Allow to rest at room temperature for 2–6 hours. Transfer the chowchow to a container and store in the refrigerator.

To make the mayo: Place the basil, chives, and parsley in a blender. Add the lemon juice and blend well. If needed, a small amount of water can be added, just enough to help the machine chop the herbs. They should end up chopped finely and dark green in color.

Using a wire whisk, combine the mayonnaise, sour cream, mustard, Tabasco, and salt in a medium bowl. Add the herb mixture and mix until completely incorporated.

To make the tomatoes: Slice the green tomatoes into thick slices, roughly 4–5 slices per tomato. In a large bowl whisk together the honey and buttermilk. Add the tomato slices and toss with your hands to coat well. Let them sit out while you make the breading.

In a large bowl mix the cornmeal, flour, sugar, and Cajun seasoning until evenly incorporated.

Coat the tomato slices in the breading and then shingle them on a baking sheet, reserving the remaining cornmeal mixture. Allow the tomatoes to rest. (Up to this point, the tomatoes could be prepared the night before and kept in the refrigerator.)

When ready to cook, pour enough canola or vegetable oil into a heavy cast-iron skillet to cover the bottom. Heat the oil over medium-high heat.

Bread the green tomatoes again in the remaining cornmeal mixture before placing them in the hot oil. Brown them evenly on both sides before removing to a paper-towel-lined plate. Immediately sprinkle lightly with kosher salt.

Serve hot, garnished with a side of chowchow and lemon herb mayo.

My Thai

1300 BANK STREET
BALTIMORE, MD 21231
(410) 327-0023
MYTHAIBALTIMORE.COM
OWNERS: BRAD WALES, VARATTAYA "PUI" WALES
CHEF: JIRAT SUPHROM-IN

My Thai is a bit like the proverbial phoenix that rose from the ashes. In December 2010, the restaurant's original location in Mount Vernon's Park Plaza Building was heavily damaged in a five-alarm fire that also destroyed the original Donna's. After a couple of years the restaurant reemerged in the Holland Tack Factory building in Baltimore's Little Italy neighborhood and is now a neighbor to Heavy Seas Alehouse.

The restaurant's new digs are spacious and handsome and, at 6,000 square feet, at least twice the size of My Thai's original basement location. In the front there's a forty-foot bar and a few tables, and a special open kitchen serving Thai street food. Beyond that, there are additional dining spaces and the semi-open main kitchen.

The Waleses' son, Jirat Suphrom-In, is in charge of the food at My Thai, especially the exotica served at the My Thai Grill Bar. This mini kitchen at the front of the restaurant was Brad Wales's idea, and a fine one it was. Where else can one find Thai street food like chicken livers with bok choy or lemongrass beef tongue with rice cakes and mango salad in Baltimore? Or fried silkworms? Yes, you read that correctly—silkworms. Actually the pupae of the *Bombyx mori,* or silk moth, fried silkworms are a crunchy snack that is quite tasty. Rather like a potato chip, actually. Except it's a bug.

Suphrom-In learned the art of Thai cooking from his mother, Pui, the restaurant's original chef. Jirat also travels to Thailand annually to study traditional methods of cooking and to pick up a new trick or dish here and there. While the street food bar is popular, drawing its own regular customers, the best sellers at My Thai are more familiar dishes like pad thai and drunken noodles.

The Waleses and Suphrom-In are quite pleased with the new location, which has seating for two hundred patrons. "We can do more things here, handling larger groups of people or events," says Suphrom-In. "I love to cook a lot of food at one time, and with this location, we're growing. The more people that walk in, the happier I am."

THAI FRIED RICE WITH CHICKEN

(SERVES 4)

1 tablespoon vegetable oil

6 ounces raw chicken, sliced

1 egg

½ cup chopped onion

1 pound cooked jasmine rice

½ cup diced tomato

2 tablespoons soy sauce

1 tablespoon sugar

½ teaspoon white pepper

Chopped scallions, for garnish

Heat the oil in a large pan over medium heat. Add the chicken and stir-fry for 1 minute or until the chicken is no longer pink.

Add the egg and chopped onion and stir for 30 seconds, then add the cooked jasmine rice, diced tomato, soy sauce, sugar, and white pepper. Stir for another 2 minutes.

Spoon onto a large platter to serve. Garnish with chopped scallions.

Note: 6 ounces raw medium shrimp may be substituted for the chicken. Cook until just opaque.

CHICKEN LETTUCE WRAPS

(SERVES 2)

6 ounces ground chicken

1 teaspoon vegetable oil

2 whole, fresh Thai chiles

1 small bunch cilantro

2 ounces minced garlic

1 tablespoon sugar

2 tablespoons fish sauce

1 tablespoon lime juice

1 ounce diced carrot

1 ounce diced red onion

1 ounce diced red and/or green bell pepper

1 head iceberg lettuce

Despite their deceptively small size, Thai chiles are very hot. Use fewer if you prefer a milder dish.

Cook the ground chicken in the oil, breaking up the meat into small pieces with a wooden spoon, until cooked through and no longer pink. Remove the chicken to a bowl.

Combine the chiles, cilantro, garlic, sugar, fish sauce, and lime juice in a blender and puree.

When the chicken has cooled, add the carrot, onion, and bell pepper. Pour the sauce over and mix well to coat the chicken and vegetables. Transfer the mixture to a serving bowl.

Cut the lettuce into quarters. Arrange on a serving plate with the bowl of chicken. Present so the diners can tear off leaves of lettuce, place a spoonful of the chicken mixture in the center of each, and fold the lettuce around it.

OF LOVE & REGRET PUB & PROVISIONS

1028 S CONKLING STREET
BALTIMORE, MD 21224
(410) 327-0760
OFLOVEANDREGRET.COM
OWNERS: BRIAN STRUMKE, BRENDA STRUMKE, LEIGH TRAVERS
CHEF: KEITH CURLEY

Brian Strumke has been called a gypsy brewer. He doesn't have a facility of his own; instead he leases space and equipment in a variety of locations, both in the United States and abroad. So if *you* were a beer savant with an amazing talent for creating new brews, what would seem to be the next logical step? No, not to open your own brewery. How about—open a restaurant?

Of Love & Regret is not just a restaurant, it is home base for Stillwater Artisanal Ales, appropriately located in the Brewer's Hill neighborhood. Strumke has said that OLAR is a "personally curated gallery for my work and the works of other artists I admire." That means that not only Stillwater beers are available on the twenty-three taps that line the wall behind the bar. Nearly half are by other American and European craft breweries, like Oxbow from Maine and Brewer's Art, a brewpub in Baltimore's Mount Vernon neighborhood that has collaborated with Strumke.

Not just a bar, Of Love & Regret is also pretty serious about the food they serve. "We want everything—from the feel of the environment, the drinks, and the food—to be about quality and artistic expression," says co-owner Brenda Strumke. The chef expressing his artistic side in the kitchen is Maryland native Keith Curley. He says his favorite things to cook are the things he grew up eating, "summer tomatoes, Silver Queen corn, local oysters, rockfish, and the mighty blue crab."

Curley's crab cake is one of the top sellers at OLAR, and the chef finds other ways to incorporate everyone's favorite crustacean into dishes, like the crab and poblano stuffing in a grilled avocado. There are snacky things like cheese plates and soft pretzels that are perfect with a beer or three. (Honestly, it's hard to get out of there without tasting several beers. Thank goodness for half pours!) But if you are looking for something more substantial, the menu options range from burgers to full-blown fork-and-knife meals like a flatiron steak or gnudi in a brown butter sauce with fresh local peas and sage.

We love Chef Curley's culinary philosophy, "Food is a part of so many moments in life, from family gatherings and celebrations to memorials. Anytime you can make someone happy through your cooking, it's a rewarding day."

Grilled Avocado with Lump Crab & Roasted Poblano Salad

(SERVES 6)

1 poblano pepper

Olive oil

3 ripe avocados

Kosher salt and black pepper

2 tablespoons mayonnaise

Juice of 1 lime

1 tablespoon minced cilantro

1 tablespoon minced basil

6 ounces jumbo lump crabmeat

Rub the poblano pepper with olive oil and grill over medium-high heat, turning frequently, until the pepper becomes soft. This should take 5–8 minutes, depending on the size of the pepper. Alternately, if you have a gas stove, place pepper directly on the burner and turn the heat to high. Using kitchen tongs, turn the pepper frequently until it is charred all over. Allow to cool and remove the stem and seeds and as much skin as will come off easily. Cut the pepper into small dice.

Split the avocado in half lengthwise and remove the pit. Rub the flesh with olive oil and season with salt and pepper. Grill over medium heat, cut side down, for 2 minutes. Remove from heat and set aside. If you don't have a grill, skip this step.

In a mixing bowl combine the mayonnaise, lime juice, cilantro, basil, and diced poblano pepper. Mix gently and add salt and pepper to taste. Fold in the crab, being careful not to break up the lumps.

Cut a small slice off the rounded skin side of the avocado halves so they will sit flat. Stuff the halves with crab salad and serve.

Oliver Speck's

507 S Exeter Street
Baltimore, MD 21202
(410) 528-8600
oliverspecks.com
Owner: Jim Lancaster
Chef: Jesse Sandlin

Most often, when there are shake-ups at a restaurant, it's because the chef has moved on to other adventures, or the business has been sold. In the case of Oliver Speck's, the chef, owner, and location are exactly the same—it's the restaurant name and concept that have changed. Vino Rosina, a wine bar serving an interesting combination of offal and a whole lotta pork (including in the cocktails), is now Oliver Speck's.

So why the change? Harbor East, which had a mere handful of restaurants fifteen years ago, is now bursting with popular eateries. But until recently, none of them served sweet tea brined chicken or BBQ ribs. Among the neighborhood's restaurants, Oliver Speck's has a more rustic vibe, for diners who are looking for something more casual and less modern American.

Ollie's, as we like to call it, is named for Chef Jesse Sandlin's pet Juliana pig. The restaurant has lost the focus on wine and somehow managed to up the pork content, as if that was even possible (remember Vino Rosina even put pork in their cocktails). It's named after a pig. The logo has a darling little piggie on it. And the menu is full of southern-style comfort food like pulled pork and spareribs. Chef Sandlin has such a fascination with the porcine protein, she even bears a pig tattoo on the top of one of her feet. "Pork is my favorite meat for a lot of reasons, mainly its versatility," she says. "It's a relatively blank canvas, and has a high fat content . . . so you can use it as a flavor vessel for whatever you'd like to do with it."

There are some non-pig-related items on the menu, like the "16-legged" burger comprising house-ground beef, bison, lamb, and pork. Oh, wait—that's pig. How about the . . . no, wait. That's pork, too. Okay, there's fried oysters and a bison pastrami Reuben, and chicken and waffles on the brunch menu. There's even something that sounds suspiciously vegetarian—mustardy pulled squash—but one never knows with Chef Jesse.

You might remember Sandlin, a Baltimore native, from her stint on *Top Chef* Season 6. Back then, the self-proclaimed culinary mercenary was top toque at Abacrombie Fine Foods. She's also worked everywhere from Australia to Sacramento, and when not heading up restaurant kitchens, she's also done work for producers like Gunpowder Bison & Trading. She's a big fan of breakfast, and believes the most important thing about cooking is to "make it taste good. That's really all there is to it."

BOURBON BREAD PUDDING

(SERVES 20)

This rich, boozy bread pudding is made even richer and boozier with an application of creamy bourbon-flavored sauce.

For the bread pudding:

10 cups bread cubes (1-inch)
1 cup golden raisins
¾ cup bourbon
3 cups heavy cream
1½ cups packed brown sugar
1 cup whole milk
8 large egg yolks
1 tablespoon vanilla extract
1½ teaspoons ground cinnamon (divided)
¼ teaspoon ground nutmeg
¼ teaspoon salt
3 tablespoons granulated sugar
6 tablespoons cold unsalted butter, cut into cubes

For the bourbon sauce:

1½ teaspoons cornstarch
¼ cup bourbon (divided)
¾ cup heavy cream
2 tablespoons granulated sugar
2 teaspoons unsalted butter, cut into small pieces
Pinch salt

To make the bread pudding: Adjust the oven rack to the middle position and preheat the oven to 450°F. Grease a 13 x 9-inch baking pan.

Spread the bread out on a baking sheet and bake until browned, about 12 minutes, turning the pieces over and rotating the baking sheet halfway through baking. Allow the bread to cool.

Reduce oven temperature to 300°F.

Warm the raisins with ½ cup of the bourbon in a small saucepan over medium-high heat until the bourbon begins to simmer, 2–3 minutes. Strain the mixture, reserving the bourbon and raisins separately.

Whisk the cream, brown sugar, milk, egg yolks, vanilla, 1 teaspoon of the cinnamon, the nutmeg, and the salt together in a large bowl. Whisk in the remaining ¼ cup bourbon and the reserved bourbon from the raisins. Toss in the toasted bread. Let the mixture sit until the bread begins to absorb the custard, about ½ hour, tossing occasionally.

Pour half of the bread mixture into the prepared baking pan, and sprinkle with half of the raisins. Repeat. Cover the pan with foil and bake for 45 minutes.

Combine the granulated sugar and the remaining ½ teaspoon of cinnamon in a small bowl. Using the fingers, work the butter into the sugar mixture until it forms lumps the size of small peas.

Remove the foil from the pudding and sprinkle with the butter mixture. Bake, uncovered, until the custard is just set, about 20–25 minutes. Increase oven temperature to 450°F and bake until the top of the pudding forms a golden crust, about 2 minutes. Transfer the pudding to a wire rack and cool for at least 30 minutes, or up to 2 hours.

To make the bourbon sauce: Whisk the cornstarch and 2 tablespoons of the bourbon together in a small bowl.

Heat the cream and granulated sugar in a small saucepan over medium heat until the sugar dissolves. Whisk in the cornstarch mixture and bring to a boil. Reduce the heat to low and cook until the sauce thickens, 3–5 minutes.

Remove from heat and stir in the remaining 2 tablespoons of bourbon, the butter, and the salt. Drizzle the warm sauce over servings of the bread pudding.

Bacon Caramel Popcorn

(SERVES 10)

Again with the bacon. What doesn't it make better?

½ cup popcorn kernels
1 pound bacon, cut into lardons and cooked until crisp
3 cups sugar
1½ tablespoons salt
3 tablespoons butter
1½ teaspoons baking soda
½ teaspoon cayenne pepper (optional)

Pop the popcorn, place it in a large bowl with the lardons, and set aside.

Line a couple of baking sheets with silicone mats or parchment paper.

Combine the sugar, salt, and butter with 1 cup water in a heavy-bottomed saucepan. Cook over medium-high heat, without stirring, until the mixture reaches between 300°F and 310°F on a candy thermometer. It's important not to stir the sugar mixture at all, as any sugar that sticks to the sides of the pan will crystallize and affect the outcome of your caramel. It's also crucial to watch the mixture as it cooks, as it can go from a perfect golden caramel to burnt and nasty in an instant.

Remove the pan from the heat and carefully add the baking soda and cayenne, if using. The mixture will foam up. Whisk until completely combined.

Pour the caramel over the popcorn and bacon and quickly mix to coat the popcorn evenly.

Spread on prepared baking sheets to cool.

PABU

725 ALICEANNA STREET
BALTIMORE, MD 21202
(410) 223-1460
PABUIZAKAYA.COM
OWNERS: MICHAEL MINA, KEN TOMINAGA
CHEF: JONAH KIM

Starting a Japanese *izakaya* (drinking establishment that serves food) in Baltimore seemed like a risky proposition. In a town not known for Japanese cuisine, going to a place that serves more than a hundred premium sakes and exotic fish flown in from Japan's fish markets might seem alien to the average Baltimorean. But Ken Tominaga is not unfamiliar with introducing Americans to the flavors of Japan. He recalls that when he opened Hana Japanese Restaurant in Sonoma County, "no one cared." It took some time to educate his customers on the difference high-quality ingredients make in the flavor of dishes. Once people tasted his food, the restaurant received critical praise and Chef Tominaga gained worldwide attention.

PABU, a semifinalist for the James Beard Foundation's Best New Restaurant 2013,

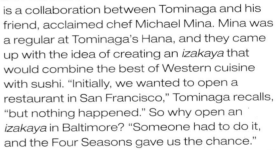

is a collaboration between Tominaga and his friend, acclaimed chef Michael Mina. Mina was a regular at Tominaga's Hana, and they came up with the idea of creating an *izakaya* that would combine the best of Western cuisine with sushi. "Initially, we wanted to open a restaurant in San Francisco," Tominaga recalls, "but nothing happened." So why open an *izakaya* in Baltimore? "Someone had to do it, and the Four Seasons gave us the chance."

PABU's menu, created by the owners and Executive Chef Jonah Kim, is an eclectic blend of Japanese ingredients with New American staples like rib eye, pork loin, and chicken wings. It's a mixing of ingredients that is startling but also makes perfect sense.

Chef Kim, who originally studied microbiology at the University of Texas, started his culinary career working at Tyson Cole's Uchi, in Austin. There he worked his way to the sushi counter, training in traditional Japanese cooking methods. He later worked in New York before landing a plum position as executive sous-chef at DJT in Vegas's Trump Hotel, which was awarded a Michelin star during his tenure there.

The balance and simplicity of Japanese food is a perfect match for Kim's culinary aesthetic. "It's the balance between texture and sweetness and spice," he says, which is evident in his Berkshire pork country ribs with red chili glaze, a perfect combination of tender meat touched with a spicy sweet sauce, and in the sweet and nutty dressing he serves with a traditional spinach side dish. He's also a fan of sourcing locally as many ingredients as possible, like poultry, which balances out those fish shipments from Japan's bustling Tsukiji Market.

For those unfamiliar with Japanese cuisine other than sushi, we highly recommend trying PABU's award-winning multicourse Satori menu, which includes sashimi, robatayaki, and what should by now be a world-famous combo of uni, oyster, and crème fraîche called the Happy Spoon. Between the great food and the incredible beverages, PABU makes us happy indeed.

BLACK PEPPER GARLIC SOY

(MAKES ABOUT 2 CUPS)

Executive Chef Jonah Kim says that this sauce is great to use on any cut of beef. At PABU, he uses the sauce on the robata skirt steak. To duplicate at home, cut skirt steak into approximately 2 x 3-inch strips and thread onto wooden skewers. Grill over high heat for a few minutes on each side, basting with some of the sauce. Offer more sauce on the side for dipping.

8 ounces soy sauce
2 ounces sake
1 ounce mirin
2 ounces toasted sesame oil
2 ounces gochujang (see Note)
½ cup sugar
6 cloves garlic, grated
1 teaspoon freshly ground black pepper

Combine all ingredients in a medium saucepan. Cook over medium heat for 10 minutes.

Note: Gochujang is a spicy, savory Korean condiment made from glutinous rice, fermented soybeans, chiles, and salt.

Goma-ae

(MAKES 2 CUPS)

Goma-ae is a simple dressing that complements steamed and blanched vegetables very well. At PABU this is paired with steamed spinach, but you can use it with any seasonal vegetable.

8½ ounces white sesame seeds
8½ ounces sugar
8 ounces soy sauce

Preheat oven to 200°F. Toast the sesame seeds for 15–20 minutes. Grind the toasted sesame seeds in a mortar and pestle.

Combine the ground sesame seeds, sugar, and soy sauce in a medium saucepan and cook until the sugar is dissolved.

Pierpoint

1822 Aliceanna Street
Baltimore, MD 21231
(410) 675-2080
Pierpointrestaurant.com
Owner: Chef Nancy Longo

Cake baker-extraordinaire Duff Goldman proclaimed Nancy Longo's crab cakes the "best thing I ever ate" on the Food Network show of the same name. He wasn't just blowing smoke—but Chef Longo does. She offers those crab cakes two ways, one traditional, the other with smoked crabmeat. It's a very subtle thing, and best noticed when the two types of cake are served side by side. In either case, it's our platonic ideal of what a crab cake should be—moist, meaty, with the crabby sweetness that comes from real blue crab.

Nancy Longo started cooking at the age of seven, at her grandmother's side. Her older sister had gone off to Europe to train as a chef, and despite her original intention of becoming a set designer, Nancy followed the same path. She spent some time as a chef instructor at her alma mater, the Baltimore International College (now Stratford University), before opening Pierpoint in 1989.

The accolades for her Fells Point eatery came pouring in from all and sundry, including *Zagat* and *Condé Nast Traveler,* and it wasn't long before Longo received a prestigious invitation to cook at the James Beard House the same year the organization nominated her for a humanitarian award. In addition, Longo has made numerous television appearances, including a feature on the late Pierre Franey's *Cooking in America* and the *Today Show.*

While owning her own restaurant has been the "fulfillment of a dream," Longo says the hours are long and all that standing does a number on one's body. That doesn't stop her from taking on numerous catering jobs as well as teaching weekend cooking classes for both adults and children.

Maryland Crab Cakes

(SERVES 4)

Chef Nancy Longo makes her famous crab cakes two ways: traditionally, with simply steamed crabmeat, or not-so-traditionally, with lightly smoked crab. The method for smoking the crab follows the recipe. We like them either way.

1 pound jumbo lump crabmeat

1 pound sweet crab claw meat

20 butter-style crackers, crushed into crumbs

2 tablespoons Dijon mustard

1 tablespoon Worcestershire sauce

2 teaspoons parsley

1 cup mayonnaise

Juice of ½ lemon

1 teaspoon dry mustard

2 eggs

1 tablespoon Old Bay seasoning

1 tablespoon salted butter, melted

To make the crab cakes: Pick through the crabmeat for bits of shell, being careful not to break up the lumps. Set aside.

Combine all of the remaining ingredients in the order listed and mix thoroughly. Add the crabmeat and gently fold in so as not to break the lumps. Form into eight approximately 4-ounce cakes. The crab cakes can be cooked either of two ways: Broil in a heated broiler in a shallow baking dish with a small amount of water for about 10 minutes, being careful not to burn them, or sauté in vegetable oil until golden brown on all sides.

To smoke the crabmeat: Soak a few fruitwood chips in a bowl of water for approximately 1 hour.

While the chips are soaking, prepare a bed of hot gray coals in a charcoal grill that has a lid. Place a small stainless steel bowl of water in the coals in the center of the grill. Remove the wet wood chips from the water and gently drop them on top of the hot coals, which will cause them to smoke.

Wrap the grill grate with a sheet of aluminum foil. Poke a few small holes in the foil, put the crabmeat on top, and set the grate in place on the grill. Cover the grill and allow the crab to smoke for approximately 30 minutes.

Remove the crabmeat from the grill and allow to cool for 1 hour. Use in the crab cake recipe in the same manner as for plain crabmeat.

It's All about the Blue Crab

Maryland is for crabs, or so the T-shirt says. And there's only one kind of crab that will pass muster in this state: the blue crab, or *Callinectes sapidus.* The moist meat from these "beautiful swimmers" has a unique savory sweetness that makes Maryland crab soup and crab cakes a year-round delicacy.

Blue crabs are native along the Atlantic coast of North and South America and in the Gulf of Mexico, but their most famous home is the Chesapeake Bay. Indeed, the town of Crisfield, Maryland, on the Eastern Shore of the Chesapeake, is known as the "crab capital of the world." The Chesapeake's crab population is in decline, however, because of years of water pollution and soil runoff from local development. Never fear! Crab fishery management programs have set standards for harvest, and currently the population is sustainable. Nevertheless, those hard crabs you're thinking about eating this weekend are likely to have come from Louisiana or North Carolina, which have more robust supplies of the beloved crustacean.

The crab recipes in this book are meant to be made with blue crab, from Maryland, if you can get it. Be aware when you're shopping for crabmeat that genuine blue crab is expensive, running $25 per pound or more. That $10 bargain crab at the local grocery store seems like a real deal, but if you look closely at the container, you won't see the word "blue" on it anywhere. Oh sure, you can still use it to make whatever crab dishes suit your fancy, but it won't be as flavorful, as sweet, as "crabby" as real blue crab.

THE RUSTY SCUPPER

402 KEY HIGHWAY
BALTIMORE, MD 21230
(410) 727-3678
SELECTRESTAURANTS.COM/RUSTY
OWNER: SELECT RESTAURANTS, INC.
CHEF: MARK MIRANDA

The Rusty Scupper has occupied its prime spot of real estate across from the busiest part of the Inner Harbor area for over thirty years now. While the area around it has changed quite a bit, with posh condos popping up next door and across the water, the Scupper has remained much the same and still has some of the best views in the area. From one side of the building, one can see Harborplace, the Promenade, and the marina, laid out as if posing for a picture postcard. The other side of the building offers a less busy view, with a wider swath of rippling water and Harbor East in the background.

The restaurant's decor can best be described as elegantly rustic, what with its heavily timbered ceiling and white tablecloths. Eating there feels like dining in a large sailing vessel, albeit one with glass walls. A favorite of visitors to the Baltimore area, the Rusty Scupper also attracts locals who want a view with their seafood. It's not only a perfect place for celebrations, including anniversaries, birthdays, and family dinners, but also for a nice evening out on the town.

Not surprisingly, seafood is the big draw at the Rusty Scupper. The menu is that of a classic Maryland seafood house—there's a shrimp cocktail, a shellfish platter—with modern touches. The executive chef, Mark Miranda, who grew up in Baltimore, has a real passion for fish and shellfish. And a good thing, too, as he goes through more than a thousand pounds of crabmeat a week in order to satisfy summertime customers hungry for classic crab cakes and stuffed shrimp, the restaurant's two top sellers.

"By living so close to the Chesapeake Bay we have access to some of the freshest seafood that is the inspiration for many of my dishes." Miranda also likes to bake. "I remember as a little boy standing on a stool and watching my mom bake. The first real book I received when I was little was a recipe book full of desserts that were easy to prepare. I spent a year going through the book and preparing each recipe. When I bake or prepare desserts, it brings back so many childhood memories." That said, we think it's necessary to save room for dessert at the Rusty Scupper.

CAJUN CRAB LINGUINE

(SERVES 1)

For the herb butter (makes 1 pound):

1¼ ounces peeled shallots
A large pinch of fresh thyme, about ⅓ teaspoon
A large pinch of fresh tarragon, about ⅓ teaspoon
5 teaspoons chopped chives
5 teaspoons chopped parsley
1 pound unsalted butter, softened
⅓ teaspoon kosher salt
⅛ teaspoon ground black pepper
1¼ teaspoons green peppercorns
5 teaspoons freshly squeezed lemon juice

For the crab linguine (per person):

3 ounces linguine
2 tablespoons olive oil
½ ounce diced red peppers
½ ounce diced yellow peppers
1 tablespoon chopped garlic
1 ounce white wine
6 ounces heavy cream
1 tablespoon Cajun blackening spice blend
2 tablespoons herb butter
2 ounces diced tomatoes
4 ounces cooked jumbo lump crabmeat
Chopped parsley, for garnish (optional)

To make the herb butter: Place the shallots, thyme, tarragon, chives, and parsley in a food processor and pulse until chopped very fine.

Place the softened butter in the bowl of a mixer. Add the chopped shallot mixture, salt, pepper, peppercorns, and lemon juice, and combine thoroughly. Be sure to scrape down the sides of the bowl to incorporate all ingredients.

Store in the freezer for up to 1 month. This recipe makes 1 pound of herb butter, for approximately 16 servings of Cajun Crab Linguine.

To make the crab linguine: Bring a large pot of salted water to a full boil. Cook the linguine al dente. Drain and, if necessary, keep hot until the sauce is done.

Meanwhile, heat the oil in a sauté pan over medium heat and add the peppers and garlic. Cook for approximately 2 minutes. Deglaze the pan with white wine and cook until reduced by half, approximately 2 minutes.

Add the cream and Cajun spice blend and cook until reduced by one-third, approximately 2 minutes. Mix in the 2 tablespoons of herb butter and the tomatoes. Add the crabmeat and combine very gently until heated, being careful not to break up the crabmeat.

Remove from heat and toss the mixture with the hot, freshly cooked and drained pasta. Serve immediately in a pasta bowl, garnishing with chopped parsley if desired. Enjoy!

SWEET POTATO CHEESECAKE

(SERVES 12)

This creamy rich dessert would make a perfect ending to a Thanksgiving dinner, don't you think?

3 pounds cream cheese, at room temperature

1 cup brown sugar

¾ cup granulated sugar

1 cup canned sweet potatoes, drained

5 whole eggs

1 teaspoon nutmeg

4 cups graham cracker crumbs

¼ pound unsalted butter, melted

1 tablespoon ground cinnamon

½ cup pecans

1 cup caramel sauce, can be store-bought or home-made

Whipped cream, for garnish

Preheat oven to 350°F.

Whip the cream cheese and both sugars in a mixer on high speed for about 10 minutes.

Mash the sweet potatoes and add to the mixture of cream cheese and sugar. Turn the speed to medium and add the eggs one at a time, waiting until each egg is fully incorporated before adding the next.

Add the nutmeg and mix until incorporated, about 2 minutes.

In a large bowl, combine the graham cracker crumbs with the melted butter and cinnamon. Press into the bottom of a 9- or 10-inch springform pan, then spray the inside of the collar with nonstick spray. Place the pan on an 18-inch-square sheet of aluminum foil and bring the edges of the foil up around the sides of the pan to form a water barrier.

Pour the cheesecake mix into the prepared springform pan and place this pan in a large roasting pan. Set the nested pans in the oven, then carefully pour hot water into the outer pan to form a water bath, about 1–2 inches up the side of the smaller pan. Make sure not to get any water in the cheesecake batter.

Bake for 1½–2 hours, checking after 1 hour and every 15 minutes after that. The cheesecake is done when a slight film has formed on the top and there is very little or no jiggling when moved.

Chop the pecans into ¼–½-inch pieces and arrange in one layer on a sheet pan. Toast in a 325°F oven for 4–5 minutes, until the nuts are crisp and lightly toasted.

Warm the caramel sauce and mix in the toasted pecans to make a praline sauce.

Cut the cheesecake into twelve pieces and drizzle praline sauce over each slice. Top with whipped cream if desired.

Salt Tavern

2127 E Pratt Street, #1
Baltimore, MD 21231
(410) 276-5480
salttavern.com
Owners: Jason Ambrose, Jane Ambrose
Chef: Brian Lavin

One of Jason Ambrose's earliest food memories was seeing his grandfather put a bit of salt on a honeydew melon, opening his eyes to what a little seasoning could do for food. Much later in life, that memory inspired the name for Ambrose's Upper Fells Point restaurant.

Ambrose acted as Salt's chef from its inception in 2006 until 2013, producing boldly flavored New American cuisine that received accolades from *Baltimore* magazine, the *City Paper,* and *Style* magazine. And then he decided he wanted out of the kitchen. Enter Brian Lavin, Salt's current chef. He was Ambrose's sous-chef for a while, so the transition has been an easy one. There are even a few dishes left over from Ambrose's tenure, perennial favorites like the Wagyu beef slider topped with foie gras and truffle aioli, and the duck fat fries. The rest of the menu is Lavin's baby, and he changes about half the dishes every two weeks or so.

Chef Lavin is from the town of Elkridge, in Howard County. He started working in restaurants as a young teen and spent time at Victoria Gastropub in Columbia and at two Wolf/Foreman restaurants, Pazo and Petit Louis, before landing at Salt. His is a minimalist approach to cuisine. "I like to use as few ingredients as possible and keep the components in a composed dish to a minimum. If you are using top-notch, fresh, and seasonal ingredients, they do most of the work themselves. It's my job to highlight them in such a way that each ingredient shows its full potential." So while his plating is unfussy, Lavin's flavors are bold, as in his salt-cod-stuffed squash blossoms, and the spiced pumpkin puree that accompanies a plate of sweetbreads.

Lest you think sweetbreads are dessert, they're the thymus or pancreas of a calf or sheep. And while the general term for animal oddments is "offal," rest assured they are anything but awful. Says Chef Levin, "Yes, the pig that produced your pork tenderloin did have a liver and the cow from which you devoured those short ribs did have a tongue, so why not use them as well? These ingredients are often more difficult to cook and take time and effort and multiple steps to execute properly, but I love to see them on menus, and they can be absolutely delicious. And more than likely you will see them on the menu at Salt."

Roasted Duck Breast with Date Puree, Roasted Parsnips & Pears & Walnut Vinaigrette

(SERVES 4)

For the duck breast:

4 (7-ounce) duck breasts, skin on
Kosher salt
Freshly ground pepper
Extra virgin olive oil

For the date puree:

½ cup minced shallots
1 tablespoon extra virgin olive oil
4 cups pitted dates
1½ cups sherry vinegar
Kosher salt, to taste

For the pears and parsnips:

3 cups peeled and diced parsnips
3 cups peeled and diced Asian pears
4 ounces melted butter
1 teaspoon ground coriander
1 teaspoon ground fennel seed
1 teaspoon ground nutmeg
Kosher salt, to taste

For the walnut vinaigrette:

½ cup minced shallots
Pinch of kosher salt
½ cup apple cider vinegar
2 cups roughly chopped toasted walnuts
1 cup extra virgin olive oil, or as needed

To make the duck breast: Gently score the skin side of the duck breasts with a sharp knife, being careful not to cut into the meat. Season the duck breasts with kosher salt and pepper on both sides.

In a lightly oiled pan over medium-low heat, place the duck breasts, skin side down. Cook for about 10 minutes, or until most of the fat has rendered out and the skin is golden brown and crispy. Flip the duck breasts and cook for an additional 3–4 minutes to achieve a medium doneness. Once the duck is cooked, remove from the pan and rest on a cutting board to let the juices redistribute throughout the meat.

To make the date puree: Gently sweat the minced shallots in a tablespoon of oil in a small pot over medium heat until they are soft, about 5 minutes. Once soft, add the pitted dates and cook for 1 minute. Deglaze the pan with the sherry vinegar; bring to a boil. Add just enough water to barely cover the dates and let simmer for about 7–10 minutes until the dates are soft. Let the date mixture cool for about 10 minutes and then, using a blender, puree the date mixture until very smooth. Season with kosher salt.

To make the parsnips and pears: Preheat oven to 350°F.

Toss all ingredients in a large bowl and season with kosher salt. Roast for about 10–12 minutes on a parchment-lined sheet tray, until the parsnips are cooked through and everything is golden brown. Halfway through cooking, rotate the tray in the oven and agitate the pears and parsnips to make sure each side is getting cooked evenly.

To make the walnut vinaigrette: Place the shallots in a bowl and season with salt. Pour the vinegar over the shallots and allow them to rest for about 15 minutes. Add the walnuts to the bowl. Whisk in enough olive oil to achieve the consistency of a chunky vinaigrette, about 1 cup. Store in an airtight container.

To assemble and serve: Spoon a pool of the date puree onto each of four warmed dinner plates. Place about 1 cup of parsnips and pears in the middle. Slice each rested duck breast on the bias into about six slices and place skin side up on the parsnips and pears. Spoon about 2 tablespoons of the vinaigrette onto each duck breast.

SoBo Cafe

6 W Cross Street
Baltimore, MD 21230
(410) 752-1518
SOBOCAFE.NET
Owner: Anna Leventis
Chef: Patrick Gramens

SoBo Cafe has been a Federal Hill stalwart for over fifteen years, even before the neighborhood became the dining hot spot it is today. A couple years back, the restaurant got itself a new owner in the form of Anna Leventis, who made a dramatic career switch from her previous life in information technology. After taking over, Leventis gussied up the place a bit but held on to the comfort food menu, which she's expanded to include more global influences. "I lived in New York for years," says Leventis, "and have had exposure to food from around the world. My favorite foods to cook and eat are international foods—Indian, Italian, Moroccan, Greek, French, Korean, Vietnamese, Thai."

Leventis's love of the exotic explains seeing a dish of merguez sausage and chickpeas (cleverly called Franks and Beans) next to pulled pork carnitas, vegetable korma, and good old American chicken pot pie on the same menu.

That pot pie, a house specialty, owes part of its popularity to the incredible crust of Patrick Gramens, the restaurant's chef, or "baker" as he likes to be called. He started out as SoBo Cafe's pastry chef, famous for the "best biscuits in town," and has now taken over the task of recipe development and general chef-ery, while sharing menu planning ideas with Leventis. Prior to taking up baking duties at SoBo, Gramens was boulanger at Bluegrass Tavern. Baking is truly a part of Gramens's heart and soul; when asked what his favorite foods are to cook and to eat, "bread" was the answer to both.

It's definitely hard to say no to the bread basket at SoBo Cafe, but do try to save some room for dinner! Soups are also popular items at the restaurant, possibly because they make a fine excuse for scarfing down still more of the crusty country-style bread.

CHICKEN POT PIE

(SERVES 6)

The secret to a terrific pot pie is the crust. Don't cheat and use something store-bought. Chef Gramens's pastry is a little more labor-intensive, but the flaky goodness is well worth the effort.

For the herb pastry:

2½ cups all-purpose flour

1 teaspoon salt

2 teaspoons sugar

¼ cup chopped herbs, like sage, rosemary, and thyme

2¼ sticks unsalted butter

1 egg, beaten

For the filling:

2 quarts chicken stock

Salt, to taste

2 pounds boneless, skinless chicken breast

2 pounds boneless, skinless chicken thighs

3 tablespoons vegetable oil

2 white onions, diced

2 large carrots, diced

2–3 ribs celery, diced

2 bay leaves

2 cloves garlic, minced

1½ cups heavy cream

1 cup cornstarch

3 small red potatoes, cut into medium dice and boiled in salted water until fork tender

1¼ cups chopped fresh sage

1 cup peas

Tabasco, to taste

To make the herb pastry: Combine the flour, salt, sugar, and herbs in a food processor. Pulse to combine. Add half of the butter and pulse until the mixture resembles a coarse meal. Tip the mixture into a mixing bowl.

Add the remaining butter to the mixing bowl and rub the butter with your hands to achieve flat pieces about the size of nickels. Add cold water, about 1 cup, a little at a time until all the flour is just hydrated. Do not over-hydrate.

Form into a flat disk and wrap in plastic wrap. Refrigerate for a minimum of 20 minutes or overnight.

Remove the dough from the refrigerator. Flour a work surface. Gently roll the dough into a 12 x 6-inch rectangle. Fold the two ends to meet in the center, and then fold the dough in half at the seam. There will be four layers. Rotate the dough a quarter turn clockwise. Roll it out to a 12 x 6-inch rectangle and repeat the four folds once again. Rotate a quarter turn clockwise again. Roll out to a 12 x 6-inch rectangle once more, this time folding the dough as you would a business letter, in 3 layers. Refrigerate 30 minutes to 1 hour.

On a floured surface, roll out to a rectangle approximately 24 x 12 inches. Dust with flour as needed. Using a pizza cutter, trim all four edges to make four right angles. Cut six equal rectangles. Refrigerate on a floured sheet pan until ready to use.

Preheat oven to 450°F. Brush the pastry with beaten egg and bake on an oiled sheet pan until puffed, golden brown, and light for its size, approximately 10–15 minutes.

To make the filling: In a large stockpot, heat the stock with salt to taste. Add the chicken and simmer until just cooked through, about 15–20 minutes. Remove the chicken to a container and reserve the stock.

In a large dutch oven, heat the oil over medium-high heat. When the oil is shimmering, add the onions, carrots, celery, and bay leaf. Cook over medium heat until the carrots are tender, then add the garlic and cook for 30 seconds. Remove the vegetables to a large bowl.

Strain the reserved stock into a pot through a fine mesh sieve. Turn on the heat, add the cream, and bring to a boil.

Make a slurry with the cornstarch and 1 cup of cold water. Whisk the slurry into the stock and boil for 1 minute until thickened. Pour the thickened stock over the reserved vegetables. Add the potatoes and the sage. Shred the chicken and add to the rest of the filling. Add the peas. Season with salt and Tabasco to taste.

To assemble the pot pies: Divide the filling among six individual single-serving casserole dishes. Top each with a rectangle of baked dough.

Ten Ten American Bistro

1010 Fleet Street
Baltimore, MD 21202
(410) 244-6867
bagbys1010.com
Owner: The Bagby Group
Chef: Chris Amendola
Pastry Chef: Bettina Perry

The old Bagby Building has become home to a trio of restaurants with distinct missions. Bagby Pizza is the place to drop in for a nice thin-crust pizza or a sandwich, Fleet Street Kitchen is a fine dining establishment, and somewhere in the middle, both physically and culinarily, is Ten Ten American Bistro. Tucked away on the courtyard of a building that was once home to a furniture factory and is on the National Register of Historic Places, Ten Ten has a rustic, postindustrial feel that reminds diners of Baltimore's history as a manufacturing town.

Ten Ten features seasonal comfort food with local Chesapeake and southern influences and a focus on fresh, locally produced ingredients and sustainable seafood. So local, some of the produce and proteins come from the Bagby Group's own Cunningham Farms in Cockeysville.

The chef at Ten Ten as well as at Fleet Street Kitchen is Chris Amendola. The two restaurants also share a pastry chef in the person of the talented Bettina Perry, whose résumé includes Bonjour Bakery, Brasserie Tatin, Blue Hill Tavern, and Linwood's. In her time here in Baltimore, she has received kudos from local media and StarChefs.com and was named 2010's Best Pastry Chef by *Baltimore* magazine.

Chef Perry grew up in the Napa Valley, where she spent lots of time in the kitchen baking cookies and pies with her mother and grandmothers. She knew from a young age that she wanted a career in food, so despite enrolling in a conventional university, she ended up with a certificate from Seattle Central Community College's specialty desserts and breads program.

Her upbringing made Bettina particularly mindful of seasonal produce. "I create seasonal desserts that elevate our guests' dining experience and really highlight the beautiful ingredients that come with each new season." As an excellent example, take her "millions of peaches" ice cream sundae, featuring both peach ice cream and peach sorbet. She also happily concocts sweet treats that use pan-seasonal ingredients like peanut butter and chocolate.

A bit of advice from us to you: When dining at either Ten Ten or Fleet Street Kitchen, make sure to leave room for dessert!

CHOCOLATE PEANUT BUTTER CUPS

(SERVES 10–12)

For the chocolate ganache:

500 grams 58% dark chocolate, cut into small pieces
500 grams heavy cream
50 grams unsalted butter

For the peanut cream:

16 ounces smooth peanut butter
8 ounces cream cheese
4 ounces unsalted butter, at room temperature
4 ounces 10x confectioners' sugar

For the Italian meringue:

16 ounces granulated sugar
8 ounces egg whites

For the chocolate peanut butter sauce:

2 cups granulated sugar
500 grams 58% dark chocolate, cut into small pieces
250 grams smooth peanut butter

For assembly:

Premade chocolate cups, about 2½-inch diameter
    (see Note)
⅓ cup lightly crushed peanut butter cereal
Peanut brittle (optional)

To make the ganache: Put the chocolate in a
heatproof bowl.

In a small saucepan, heat the cream just until
it comes to a boil. Pour the cream over the
chocolate in the bowl. Let stand for 1–2 minutes
to melt the chocolate.

Add the butter and whisk the mixture until
smooth.

To make the peanut cream: Combine the
ingredients in a stand mixer with paddle
attachment and beat until smooth, light, and
creamy. Set aside.

To make the meringue: Place the sugar in a
saucepan and add enough water to dampen it.
Cook over medium-high heat without stirring until
it reaches the soft ball stage, or when a candy
thermometer reads 240°F.

While the sugar is cooking, put the egg whites in a stand mixer with whisk attachment and whisk at medium speed. When sugar is at temperature, slowly pour it into the egg whites, still at medium speed. When the sugar is incorporated, turn the speed up to high and whip until the mixing bowl is cool to the touch.

Spoon the meringue into a pastry bag.

To make the chocolate peanut butter sauce: Combine the sugar with 2 cups of water in a saucepan and cook until the sugar is completely dissolved, creating a simple syrup.

Place the chocolate and peanut butter in a heatproof bowl.

Pour the simple syrup over the chocolate and peanut butter and stir until the chocolate melts and becomes a sauce.

To assemble: Fill each of the premade chocolate cups half full with the peanut cream.

Top the peanut cream with a layer of crushed peanut butter cereal. Fill the rest of the cup with ganache and allow to set.

When cool, pipe a swirl of meringue on top of the filled cup. Using a crème brûlée torch, gently brown the meringue without melting the chocolate underneath.

Garnish each plate with a drizzle of chocolate peanut butter sauce and set a meringue-topped peanut butter cup in the center. Add small pieces of peanut brittle, if desired.

Note: Premade chocolate cups can be purchased online.

THAMES STREET OYSTER HOUSE

1728 THAMES STREET
BALTIMORE, MD 21231
(443) 449-7726
THAMESSTREETOYSTERHOUSE.COM
OWNER: CANDACE BEATTIE
CHEF: ERIC HOUSEKNECHT

At first glance, Thames Street Oyster House appears to be a typical Fells Point seafood restaurant. Rowhouse location facing the water? Check. Exposed brick walls? Check. New England lobster roll and grilled linguiça sausage? Wait—huh? Where are the traditional Maryland favorites, the crab cakes and crab soup? Look closer, they're definitely there, hidden among the several New England seafood specialties that pepper the menu.

It's actually a perfectly sensible concept, combining our local cuisine with that of parts north. Both Maryland and New England are known for scrumptious seafood, so why not offer diners the best of both worlds? So was the thought behind Thames Street Oyster House. Owner Candace Beattie and Executive Chef Eric Houseknecht are both native Marylanders. Both spent time living and eating up and down New England, and both ended up moving back to the Baltimore area.

While oysters are an obvious focus at the Oyster House—available fried, a la Rockefeller, in stew, and on the half shell—seafood in general is the star of the show. And there are definite Maryland influences. Snuggled between the Gulf of Maine Hake and Grilled New Bedford Swordfish listings in the main course section of the menu is that crab cake, Eastern Shore style, made with real East Coast blue crab, and served in a little cast-iron pan. The crab soup is made with short ribs, the way the chef's grandmother made it.

Chef Eric Houseknecht grew up in Carroll County. He started working in restaurants at the age of fourteen, and after watching the cooks do their thing in the kitchen, Eric became interested in food and cooking. He left Maryland to attend culinary school at Johnson & Wales University in Providence, Rhode Island, and hung around in the area for a while, working as sous-chef at Mills Tavern in Providence before coming back to Maryland. Here he was chef de cuisine at Salt Tavern before opening Thames Street Oyster House with Candace. A mutual friend introduced the two. "Eric is an outstanding chef," says Beattie. "Without him, this restaurant would not be what it is."

Rhode Island Quahog Chowder

(SERVES 8)

Chef Houseknecht says, "This was the first soup I learned how to make when I moved to Providence. It still always reminds me of cold rainy days and fishing in New England." The word "quahog," by the way, is pronounced "co-hog" and refers to a large hard-shell clam.

6 quahog clams or 2 cups chopped clams
1 cup diced applewood-smoked bacon
1 medium Spanish onion, diced
4 stalks celery, diced
Kernels from 3 ears fresh corn
3 tablespoons all-purpose flour
3 cups diced red potatoes
1 quart fresh or bottled clam juice
2 bay leaves
2 cups cream
1 teaspoon fresh chives
1 teaspoon fresh thyme
Salt and pepper

Open the clams over a bowl, reserving the juices. Remove the clam meat from the shells and slice thinly. Keep the sliced clams and juices in a bowl until ready to use.

In a soup pot, render the diced bacon until crispy. Add the onion, celery, and corn, and cook until the vegetables soften. Stir in the flour and mix well.

Add the potatoes, clam juice, bay leaves, and 1 cup of water to the pot. Bring to a simmer and cook until the potatoes are soft, about 20 minutes.

Stir in the clams and their liquid, the cream, and the herbs. Simmer for 15 minutes. Add salt and pepper to taste.

At approximately two hundred miles long and covering 4,479 square miles (including its tributaries), the Chesapeake Bay is the largest estuary in the United States. An estuary is a body of water that is formed when rivers and streams flow into an ocean. This mixing of fresh and salt waters creates a salinity within the Chesapeake that makes it the perfect home for oysters. And oysters, natural water filters that each clean about fifty gallons of water per day, are the perfect residents for the bay. Nature had a great system going there, and then humans showed up and ruined everything when they determined that (1) oysters are delicious and (2) the bay is a great place to dump everything from chemical runoff to chicken poop. The resulting combination of overharvesting and pollution damaged the bay's ecosystem and devastated the oyster population.

Fortunately this was realized before it was (too) too late. In 1967 the Chesapeake Bay Foundation was formed to find solutions to the region's pollution problems. About twenty years ago the Oyster Recovery Partnership was commissioned to restore the oyster population. The ORP has planted nearly four billion oysters on 1,500 acres of oyster reefs, and nearly 30,000 bushels of shell have been recycled to provide homes for new oysters. Also, new oyster farms are popping up here and there, not only restoring the bay's natural filtration system but also supplying restaurants with the briny bivalves, because oysters are still delicious.

Unlike other farmed seafoods that create ecological issues of their own, farmed oysters are environmentally restorative, and they account for 95 percent of the oysters consumed worldwide. The Monterey Bay Aquarium's Seafood Watch program has recommended oysters as a Best Choice in sustainable seafood, so what are you waiting for? Go eat some oysters!

Tooloulou

4311 Harford Road
Baltimore, MD 21214
(443) 627-8090
TOOLOULOU.COM
Owners: Chef Shawn Lagergren, Megan Lagergren

From the outside, the tiny storefront on Harford Road in the Arcadia neighborhood of northern Baltimore City looks like a typical carryout. But that's where the similarities end. Sure, they serve pizzas at Tooloulou, but they're crispy, thin-crust artisan pizzas with creative toppings like smoked duck or alligator. We've personally been driven to the brink of insanity by the fragrance wafting out of a box containing a pizza called the Tooloulou, topped with crab, andouille sausage, peppers, and Old Bay, and debated ripping into it on the five-mile drive back to our house. Five miles is too far for such torture, but Tooloulou is so tiny—just a couple of tables and stools for dining in—parties of more than one or two people do well to take their food home.

The owners of this tiny gem are Louisiana native Chef Shawn Lagergren and his wife, Megan. At four years of age, Shawn started cooking with his grandmother, who schooled him in classic French technique. By the age of twelve, Shawn had decided that he wanted to open a restaurant. Before that happened, he moved to Baltimore and worked at restaurants like Dionysus and City Cafe. Tooloulou, which is Cajun for "crab," opened in 2012 and showcases the bayou flavors Lagergren grew up with.

"The food scene in Hamilton/Lauraville/Arcadia is full of trailblazers. We felt the neighborhood could use an artisan pizza place. Our goal was to do good food that

people could stop in and get on the way home from work and eat on a regular basis. Cajun food is a big part of what I love to cook, so we added in the po'boys and other dishes to reflect that."

Those po'boys include your choice of fillings, like fried oysters, roast beef, or gator, all "dressed proper" with lettuce, tomato, spicy Cajun pickles, and Tabasco remoulade, on crisp French bread. The fried shrimp po'boy is a big seller, as is the sandwich made with Coca-Cola baked ham on a gigantic cheddar jalapeño biscuit. Try it with a side of Maw Maw's potato salad, made from his grandmother's secret recipe.

"There is passion and history in the food I cook, and I want others to get excited about what I'm making. Food and cooking are a way of life; it's comforting and full of emotion. I'm not so worried about food trends but more about using local and fresh ingredients that will help my dishes to be the best they can be."

MARYLAND CRAB CHOWDER

(SERVES 6–8)

There are generally two kinds of crab soup served in Maryland: the vegetable-soup-based version, or a flour-thickened creamy version. At Tooloulou, it's more like a chowder, with minimal vegetables and chunks of potato.

1 cup unsalted butter
2 tablespoons fresh minced garlic
2 medium yellow onions, finely chopped
1 stalk celery, finely chopped
½ cup flour
½ cup crab stock or seafood stock
1 teaspoon salt
1 teaspoon pepper
2 bay leaves
1 teaspoon fresh thyme
5 Yukon Gold potatoes, cut in medium dice
1 quart heavy cream
1 pound fresh Maryland lump crabmeat
2 tablespoons Old Bay seasoning

In a 2-quart pot, melt the butter over medium heat. Add the garlic, onion, and celery, cooking until the onions and celery are soft. Add the flour and cook for 2 minutes, stirring frequently.

Add the crab stock and enough water to fill the pot to within 2 inches of the top. Add the seasonings and cook, stirring frequently, for 20 minutes, being careful not to let the ingredients stick to the bottom.

Add the potatoes and cook for an additional 20 minutes, stirring frequently.

Slowly stir in the heavy cream, and finally add the crabmeat. Cook until the soup is thickened and the potatoes are soft. Season to taste. Remove the bay leaves before serving.

Serving option: Add additional crabmeat to the serving bowls, ladle in the soup, and sprinkle with Old Bay.

surprisingly, Waterfront Kitchen hosts a number of wine dinners, some of which occur after a cruise around the harbor in a sailing vessel, as part of the Living Classrooms Tall Ship program. And the fun doesn't stop there. Chef Pellegrino also loves to share his wealth of culinary knowledge, so he offers myriad cooking classes on Mondays and Thursdays, on subjects ranging from soup making to grilling poultry to molecular gastronomy.

Does the man ever sleep?

WATERFRONT KITCHEN SUMMER CORN CHOWDER

(SERVES 4)

This soup is best when made with freshly picked corn.

6 ears fresh sweet corn

1 tablespoon unsalted butter

1 bacon strip, chopped

1 small yellow onion, chopped

1 carrot, peeled and chopped

1 celery stalk, chopped

3½ cups heavy cream

1 bay leaf

1 medium Yukon Gold potato, peeled and diced

1 red bell pepper, chopped

Salt and freshly ground black pepper

½ teaspoon fresh tarragon leaves

Shuck the corn and blanch the ears in a large pot of boiling water for 4 minutes. Plunge into ice water to cool, then cut the kernels from the cobs and reserve.

In a large saucepan, melt the butter over medium heat. Add the bacon and fry until it renders its fat but doesn't begin to brown. Add the onion and sauté for 4–5 minutes, until soft. Add the carrot and celery and cook for 4–5 minutes more. Add the heavy cream and bay leaf. Bring to a boil and reduce heat to a bare simmer. Cover the pot and cook for 30 minutes, stirring occasionally to prevent the cream from burning on the bottom of the pot.

Add the reserved corn kernels along with the potato, bell pepper, and salt and pepper to taste. Bring to a simmer and reduce the heat to maintain the simmer for 15 minutes, or until the potatoes are almost fork tender. Add the tarragon and serve hot.

When Jo Cosgrove volunteered to help build the greenhouse on a plot of land on Caroline Street to assist with the Living Classrooms BUGS program, she never expected to be named full-time gardener. Jo had worked in the hospitality industry for some time and was working for Waterfront Kitchen when they decided to put her in charge of tending the garden and greenhouse that not only provides valuable skills to inner-city children but serves as a source of ingredients for the restaurant.

The new greenhouse is three times the size of the original structure and complements the four raised beds and chicken coop already on the premises. Originally the site of a propeller factory, this urban garden produces a plethora of vegetables and herbs including six varieties of tomato, squash, lima beans, cucumbers, beets, fennel, radishes, and microgreens. It even supplies ornamental plants for decorating the restaurant, like black-eyed Susans.

The students who work in the garden come from areas where they would not normally have exposure to such agricultural experiences. Jo teaches the children such things as compatible planting, where certain plants are grown together for mutual benefit. For example, marigolds serve to keep pests away from sweet potatoes.

It's not just the children who can learn from this project. The restaurant offers Sunday afternoon classes for those who want to improve their own gardening skills. Classes on watering techniques, composting, and building raised beds are also taught at the greenhouse.

THE WINE MARKET

921 E FORT AVENUE
BALTIMORE, MD 21230
(410) 244-6166
WINEMARKETBISTRO.COM
OWNER: CHRISTOPHER SPANN
CHEF: KEVIN CHRISTIAN

The Wine Market is a seven-day-a-week wine and spirits shop with more than eight hundred wines for sale along with a wide selection of specialty beers and spirits. It leans toward smaller producers who favor quality grapes and place of origin over fussy winemaking trickery. It's a great place to buy wine, but it's even better when you enjoy some of their wines with food prepared in their restaurant.

Chef Kevin Christian, who worked at Tersiguel's in Ellicott City before coming to the Wine Market, likes to focus on quality ingredients that are local and sustainable. "My personal culinary philosophy is to use as few ingredients as I can and make them each shine."

The interior of the bistro feels a bit like a loft in lower Manhattan, and this casual vibe translates to the food. The menu is divided into starters, small plates, mid plates, and entrees, with wine pairing recommendations, so there are options no matter how hungry you are or how much you want to spend. "I think the dining scene is becoming more progressive each year," says Chef Christian, "in that it's filled with people who don't necessarily have deep pockets but want to eat good food."

The menu is largely straightforward American cuisine, but with a great deal of care placed on the details. "My favorite things to cook are things that require the hard labor of cooking, like pasta for instance. I also love food that you have to cure and grind and wait to see what the results are in a couple of weeks." And the menu evolves depending on which ingredients are in season. Even during Restaurant Week, the bistro reserves the right to change the prix-fixe menu based on the best ingredients available. "The most popular dishes at the Wine Market change because the menu changes all the time," Chef Christian points out.

Broccoli Ravioli with Short Rib, Capers & Anchovy

(SERVES 5)

For the short ribs:

5 pounds short ribs
2 tablespoons cooking oil
1 Spanish onion, roughly chopped
1 carrot, peeled and roughly chopped
2 celery stalks, roughly chopped
¼ cup tomato paste
½ bottle dry red wine
3 quarts chicken broth

For the ravioli:

3 heads broccoli, cut into florets
1 pound ricotta
Zest of 1 lemon
½ pound pasta dough

For assembly:

4 tablespoons butter
¼ cup capers
1 tablespoon chopped anchovies
1½ pounds braised short rib meat, chopped
3 tablespoons lemon juice
½ bunch parsley, finely chopped
Salt and pepper, to taste
Grated Parmesan cheese

To make the short ribs: Preheat oven to 300°F.

Heat the oil in a lidded, ovenproof pan and sear the short ribs on both sides until golden brown, about 5 minutes per side. Remove from heat and set aside.

Cook the onion, carrot, and celery in the same pan until they are nicely caramelized. Add the tomato paste and cook, stirring frequently, for 1–2 minutes. Deglaze the pan with the red wine and reduce until it is almost evaporated, scraping the pan as it reduces. Next add the chicken stock and bring to a simmer.

Put the short ribs back into the pan and transfer to the preheated oven. Cook for about 3–3½ hours or until tender. Remove from heat and allow to cool.

When the ribs are cool enough to handle, remove the meat from the bones and break into small pieces. Set aside 1½ pounds for this recipe.

To make the ravioli: Bring a pot of salted water to a boil and add the broccoli. Once the broccoli is tender, about 3 minutes, shock it in a bowl of ice water. Place the broccoli in a blender and puree until smooth. Turn out the puree onto several layers of cheesecloth and hang it for at least 3 hours or up to a day. Combine the puree with the ricotta and add the lemon zest. Season with salt and pepper and keep cold. When ready to use, scoop the puree into a pastry bag fitted with a plain round tip.

Bring the pasta dough to room temperature. Cut it in half and wrap one half in plastic wrap. Dust the unwrapped portion with flour. Flatten it with your hands as much as you can. Place the dough on the widest setting of your pasta roller and run it through. Run it through twice more. Fold the dough double and run it through to get a nice square piece. Run it through each setting until you reach the smallest. Flour a large prep surface and lay the pasta sheet over it. Using a spray bottle, spritz the pasta sheet lightly with water.

Find the midpoint of the pasta sheet and mark it. On the right-hand half of the pasta sheet, use the pastry bag to squeeze 1-tablespoon dollops of the filling mixture, beginning 1 inch to the right of the midline and 1 inch from the top, and placing additional dollops at 2-inch intervals. Fold the left side of the pasta sheet on top of the right side and use your fingers to seal the pasta around each mound of filling. Cut out the individual

2-inch squares using either a pasta cutter or a knife. Once formed, you can move the ravioli to a floured sheet tray and into the freezer.

Repeat with the other half of the pasta dough.

To assemble: Bring a pot of salted water to a boil. Add the ravioli to the pot. Cook 3–4 minutes, until tender. Drain, reserving 1 cup of the pasta water.

Heat the butter in a large sauté pan. Once the butter foams, add the capers, anchovies, and reserved short rib meat. Add the cooked ravioli to the pan along with a bit of the pasta water, tossing lightly until a sauce has formed. Add the lemon juice and parsley and season with salt and pepper.

Divide the ravioli among five plates, spooning over some of the sauce and meat, and sprinkle on a little Parmesan.

Braised Pork Cheeks with Ramp Puree, Fava Beans, Marble Potatoes & Pickled Ramps

(SERVES 4)

For the pork cheeks:

4 (8-ounce) pork cheeks
Salt and pepper
3 tablespoons vegetable oil for frying
½ cup Worcestershire sauce
8 cups chicken stock
2 cups pineapple juice
¼ cup soy sauce
½ cup balsamic vinegar

For the potatoes:

1½ pounds marble potatoes

For the ramp puree:

1 pound ramps, cleaned, white root ends
    reserved for pickles
1 bunch chives
½ bunch cilantro
1 garlic clove
½ cup olive oil
Salt and pepper
Lemon juice, to taste

For the pickled ramps:

Reserved ramp root ends
Champagne vinegar
Sugar
1 cinnamon stick
1 tablespoon coriander seeds
1 fresno chile, deseeded and sliced

For the fava beans:

2 pounds fresh fava beans
Kosher salt
1 teaspoon olive oil
1 teaspoon unsalted butter

For serving:

2 tablespoons unsalted butter
1 tablespoon olive oil
A few tablespoons of chicken stock

To make the pork cheeks: Preheat an oven to 300°F.

Season the pork cheeks liberally with salt and pepper. Heat the oil in a large sauté pan. Sear the cheeks on both sides until nicely browned.

Place the cheeks in a large baking pan. Add the Worcestershire, chicken stock, pineapple juice, soy sauce, and vinegar. Bring the liquid to a boil on the stovetop, then cover the pan and place it the oven. Cook for 2½–3 hours.

To make the potatoes: Place the potatoes in a pot, cover with 2 inches of cold water, and bring to a simmer. When the potatoes are just tender, about 15–20 minutes, shock them in a bowl of ice water. Once cool, drain them and cut them into medium dice.

To make the ramp puree: Bring a large pot of salted water to a boil. Blanch the ramp greens for about 30 seconds, then shock them in a bowl of ice water. Do the same with the chives and the cilantro.

Place the blanched ramp greens and herbs in a blender along with the garlic, and puree, slowly drizzling in the olive oil. When combined, pour the mixture into a bowl and season it with salt, pepper, and lemon juice to taste.

To make the pickled ramps: Place the white root end of the ramps in a bowl and add water until it just covers the ramps. Pour the water into a measuring cup and note the volume. Measure out that much champagne vinegar and pour it and the water used to cover the ramps into a pot. Wipe out the measuring cup and pour in sugar to equal half the volume of the vinegar. Add that to the pot. Tie the cinnamon stick, coriander seeds, and fresno chile in a piece of cheesecloth with butcher's twine and add that to the pot. Bring the mixture to a boil and pour it over the ramp ends. Set the bowl with the pickled ramp mixture over a larger bowl filled with ice to cool.

To make the fava beans: Shell the beans. Bring 4 quarts of water to a boil. Add enough salt to make the water taste like seawater. Add the beans and cook for about 3 minutes.

When beans are done, remove from boiling water and shock in a bowl of ice water. Allow them to cool, then remove from water and peel off outer skin.

In a skillet, combine butter and oil over medium heat. Add peeled favas and sauté for 5–7 minutes, until done to your liking. Keep warm until ready to serve.

To serve: In a sauté pan, simmer the cooked pork cheeks and a small amount of the braising liquid. Once the liquid starts to reduce, add 1 tablespoon of unsalted butter and spoon the mixture over the cheeks to glaze them.

Heat the olive oil in another sauté pan and add the fava beans and diced marble potatoes. Stir gently until warmed through. Add 1 tablespoon of butter and a few tablespoons of chicken stock to make a glaze for the vegetables.

To assemble, smear some of the ramp puree on each of four plates. Add the fava beans and potatoes in a pile in the center. Place a pork cheek on top of the vegetables and drizzle with some of the pan sauce. Garnish with some of the pickled ramp bottoms.

Wit & Wisdom

200 International Drive
Baltimore, MD 21202
(410) 576-5800
WITANDWISDOMBALTIMORE.COM
Owner: Michael Mina
Chef: Zack Mills

Multiple James Beard Award–winning chef Michael Mina has one overriding philosophy: "Balance in everything creates memories and experiences." From the time he opened his San Francisco restaurant Aqua in 1991 to much acclaim, Mina has focused on creating memorable dining experiences, and he has done so successfully with his array of restaurants across the country. In recent years Mina has brought his impressive culinary skills to bear on two Baltimore restaurants in the Four Seasons Hotel: PABU and Wit & Wisdom.

Wit & Wisdom is the main restaurant for the hotel, serving breakfast, lunch, and dinner for its guests, but also providing a tavern-style experience for everyone who dines there. The live-fire grill and rotisserie are plainly visible to the diners as is the breathtaking view of the harbor. Their menu of comfort food has a definite Eastern Seaboard slant, with dishes like Amish organic chicken, Piedmont Ridge smoked roasted rib eye, and Ocean City black sea bass. There's even a blue crab tasting entree featuring crab cake, soft-shell crab, and spicy tomato crab stew.

Mina tapped Zack Mills, a native Marylander and graduate of the French Culinary Institute, to run the kitchen at Wit & Wisdom after a stint overseeing culinary operations for several of Mina's restaurants. Previously at Bourbon Steak in Washington, DC, Mills brings his wealth of local cuisine knowledge to the Mina philosophy of cooking. "With my close ties to the community, I've been able to maintain strong relationships with the area's top farms and look forward to continuing to grow the restaurant's relationships with

regional purveyors." His menu at Wit & Wisdom features bold flavors that are balanced and keep diners interested throughout the course.

Two of the best-selling dishes at Wit & Wisdom are that Maryland Crab Tasting (which Mills refers to as a "greatest hits" of Maryland blue crab) and the local rockfish. "I'm happy that these tend to be our best sellers as they are both synonymous with our area and are dishes that we developed to showcase the state's amazing seafood offerings."

MARYLAND CRAB SOUP
(SERVES 8)

A recipe from Chef Mills's family, this soup is featured in the restaurant's Maryland Crab Tasting.

½ pound Roma tomatoes
Olive oil
Salt and pepper, to taste
4¼ cups shellfish or fish stock
4¼ cups tomato juice
1 tablespoon diced jalapeño, with seeds
¼ pound Yukon Gold potatoes, diced
1 teaspoon finely minced chipotle pepper
1 garlic clove, minced
1 bay leaf
½ teaspoon thyme
1½ teaspoons lemon juice
1 teaspoon Old Bay seasoning
½ teaspoon salt

For the garnish:

2 cups jumbo lump crabmeat
2 cups raw corn kernels
1 cup pearl onions, halved
1½ cups English peas, blanched
1 cup celery leaves

Cut the tomatoes in half, brush with olive oil, season with salt and pepper, and place on a grill, cut side down. until nicely charred. Turn and cook on the skin side for about 1 minute and remove.

In a soup pot over medium heat, combine the shellfish stock, tomato juice, charred tomatoes, jalapeño, diced potato, chipotle, and garlic. Tie up the bay leaf and thyme in a piece of cheesecloth and add to the pot as well.

Bring the soup to a simmer and cook for about 45 minutes, or until the soup is reduced by one-third and the potatoes are fully cooked.

While the soup is cooking, combine the garnish ingredients in a bowl. Set aside.

Discard the cheesecloth bundle, transfer the soup to a blender in batches, and blend until smooth. Season with lemon juice and Old Bay. Strain the solids out of the soup and discard. Return the soup to the pot. Add the garnish and heat over medium heat until warmed through.

Serve with crab toast.

CRAB TOAST

(MAKES 8–10)

1 red bell pepper

1 fresno chile

Zest and juice of 1 orange

Juice of 1 lemon

1 egg yolk

⅓ cup toasted panko bread crumbs

½ cup garlic oil

½ cup jumbo lump crabmeat

1 tablespoon minced chives

1 baguette, sliced ¾-inch thick

Char the bell and fresno peppers on a burner or grill until the skins are black. Transfer to a bowl and cover with plastic to steam for 5 minutes. Remove the peppers' skins and seeds.

Preheat oven to 400°F.

Place the peppers in a food processor with the orange zest and juice, lemon juice, egg yolk, and bread crumbs. Puree the mixture while slowly drizzling in the oil.

Transfer the mixture to a mixing bowl and fold in the crabmeat and chives.

Spread the mixture baguette slices and place in the 400°F oven for 5 minutes.

Woman's Industrial Kitchen

333 N Charles Street
Baltimore, MD 21201
(410) 244-6450
WOMANSINDUSTRIALKITCHEN.COM
Owner: Irene Smith

The Woman's Industrial Exchange has a long and storied history. It started shortly after the Civil War as a consignment shop for women's handiwork and a means of helping women in need earn a discreet living. Exchanges were opened around the country as the movement grew; as many as seventy-two existed by 1891. Eventually there was a decline, and today there are about twenty left. Only a handful date from the nineteenth century, including Baltimore's Exchange, which continues its mission as an outlet for men and women to support themselves with handcrafted goods.

Originally founded in the home of one Mrs. G. Harmon Brown, the Exchange moved into its current location, which is on the National Register of Historic Places, in 1887. The rear part of the building, behind the storefront, became a lunchroom that over the years was best known for its chicken salad sandwiches served with tomato aspic and deviled eggs, as well as for the charming elderly ladies who served as waitresses. One of them, Marguerite Schertle, who appeared in the 1993 movie *Sleepless in Seattle* starring Meg Ryan and Tom Hanks, worked at the Exchange until she was ninety-five.

Eventually the lunchroom fell on some hard times and closed in 2002. After a couple of fits and starts, it reopened in its current incarnation, the Woman's Industrial Kitchen, in 2011. The Kitchen's proprietor and chef is Irene Smith, a seemingly tireless champion for human rights, truth, justice, the American way, and women's rights. She also runs the popular Souper Freak food truck.

About the restaurant, Smith says, "This place is unique in the world. It's the only restaurant dedicated to women's history." That history can be seen all around. While the black and white tile floors of the lunchroom of yore are still intact, the dining room has been gussied up with a coat of shocking pink paint, and the walls and tabletops are decorated with images of notable women. Many are Marylanders like Gertrude Stein, Emily Post, and Billie Holiday.

"Teachers, poets, writers, athletes, musicians all nourish us," says Smith. And she nourishes us too, with her menu of comfort foods that include that famous tomato aspic

and chicken salad, along with a few modern touches. Irene's soups are legendary, and in the summertime there's usually a version of gazpacho using whatever vegetables Irene has picked up from local farmers that week. "Farming, locally sourced foods, work, waitressing, cooking, history—they are all valuable. Our legacy can't be microwaved dinners."

CHARLOTTE RUSSE

(SERVES 8)

It is said that the French chef Antonin Carême made the first Charlotte Russe to honor both the daughter of a former employer (Princess Charlotte of Wales) and his current employer (Czar Alexander, a Russian). All we know is that it's a fairly classic icebox-type cake, with a filling of flavored whipped cream within a mold lined with ladyfingers and topped with fresh fruit—and delicious.

For the ladyfingers:

½ cup unsalted butter
1 cup white sugar
½ cup heavy whipping cream
1 tablespoon vanilla extract
1¾ cups all-purpose flour
½ teaspoon baking powder

For the filling:

⅓ cup unflavored gelatin powder
¼ cup milk, at room temperature
2½ cups heavy cream
1½ cups sugar
2 tablespoons vanilla extract
7 egg whites

For assembly:

Fresh berries

To make the ladyfingers: Cream the butter, sugar, cream, and vanilla until fluffy and light.

Sift the flour and baking powder together. Add the flour mixture to the creamed butter with a spatula. Mix slowly until totally incorporated. Refrigerate for 1 hour.

Preheat the oven to 350°F.

Put the batter in a pastry bag fitted with a ½-inch plain round tip, or, if using a plastic bag, cut a corner off, leaving a ½-inch opening.

Line a cookie sheet with parchment paper. Pipe the batter onto the paper in six ½ x 5-inch strips. Grease a 9 x 2-inch round baking pan and squeeze the remaining batter into it.

Place both pans in the preheated oven. Bake for 10–15 minutes, until the fingers are golden brown and spring back lightly when touched. Remove from the oven and allow to cool completely.

Cut the ladyfingers in half. Each piece should measure about 2 x 2½ inches.

To make the filling: Sprinkle the gelatin into a bowl. Add the milk and stir gently with a silicone spatula until the gelatin is absorbed and appears granular.

Beat the cream and sugar together until stiff. Add the vanilla and beat an additional 3 minutes. Add the gelatin and milk mixture and beat an additional 5 minutes.

In a separate bowl, beat the egg whites until slightly stiff peaks form. Using a silicone spatula, fold the egg whites gently into the whipped cream mixture.

To assemble: Set out a 9-inch springform pan, or line a 9-inch cake pan with foil so the foil sticks up above the pan and forms handles.

Place the round cake layer in the bottom of the prepared pan. Arrange the ladyfingers in a ring around the edge of the pan, rounded side out. Gently pour the mixture of cream and egg whites into the pan, making sure not to knock down any of the ladyfingers. Smooth the top with a spatula or knife. Arrange berries decoratively around top.

Chill for at least 12 hours, or until completely set.

Remove the collar from the springform pan and cut the cake into slices. If using a foil-lined pan, it helps to have another set of hands to hold the pan steady as you lift the cake out by the handles.

Tomato Aspic

(SERVES MANY, DEPENDING ON THEIR APPETITE FOR ASPIC)

This looks best if made in a decorative gelatin mold. If you don't have a mold, a small bundt pan will work just fine, but a 9 x 5-inch baking pan is good, too.

½ cup unflavored gelatin powder
8 cups stewed tomatoes
4 celery stalks with leaves
4 carrots
½ onion
2 teaspoons black pepper
2 teaspoons Old Bay seasoning
2 bay leaves
½ teaspoon cloves
1 teaspoon salt
Release spray

In a small dish, soften the gelatin with 1 pint of cold water. Stir with a silicone spatula until the gelatin is smooth and has absorbed the water. Set aside.

Combine the vegetables and seasonings in a large pot with 3 pints of warm water. Boil rapidly, stirring frequently, for 40–50 minutes. The vegetables should be very soft and the tomatoes mostly broken down.

Strain the tomato mixture into a large bowl. Repeat. There should be no particulate matter in the liquid. It should look, smell, and taste a bit like V-8. Immediately stir in the softened gelatin, continuing to stir with the silicone spatula until all the gelatin is dissolved.

Pour into a mold. If using a decorative mold, spray first with release spray.

Refrigerate for at least 4 hours, or until completely set.

Ze Mean Bean

1739 FLEET STREET
BALTIMORE, MD 21231
(410) 675-5999
ZEMEANBEAN.COM
OWNER: YVONNE DORNIC
KITCHEN MANAGER: JIM RHODES

The neighborhood of Fells Point served as the port of Baltimore for many years and was second only to Ellis Island in the number of immigrants that landed in the United States in the nineteenth and early twentieth centuries. Many of those émigrés were from Eastern Europe—Poland, Ukraine, Czechoslovakia—and a good number of them settled in the neighborhood. Soon storefronts bore the names Ostrowski and Macek and Simek, and area churches offered handmade pierogi to those too busy to make the labor-intensive dumplings at home.

While Fells Point's population has changed over the years, one can still find Slavic specialties like *holupki* (stuffed cabbage), *placki* (potato pancakes), and kielbasa at Ze Mean Bean. Yvonne Dornic opened the cafe, a Fells Point take on an Eastern European coffeehouse, in 1995 as an ode to her Slovakian father, Ivan (shown here), serving desserts made by her mother, Ann. "Our guests loved the coziness and eclectic vibe of the cafe immediately. Very quickly our clientele made this an evening hot spot, enjoying our candlelit dining room, live entertainment, monthly art showing and BYOB policy. However, as we grew, our guests requested more sophisticated dinner options and a wider array of drink selections. So, we listened to them. Three years in, we applied for our liquor license, expanded our menu and doubled the size of our small dining room by adding a second floor and private dining room."

Ze Mean Bean's Slavic specialties, "family recipes handed down through the generations and prepared with love by our Eastern European cooks who have their origins in Slovakia, Poland, and Ukraine," are a big draw; the beet-based Ukrainian

borscht is a particular favorite of ours. But for the patrons who aren't homesick for Eastern Europe, Dornic and Managing Partner/Kitchen Manager Jim Rhodes have incorporated some new American elements into the menu, like crab-crusted mahimahi and curried quinoa cakes. Mama Ann still makes all of the desserts, though, including a mean chocolate babka.

After nineteen years of fine-tuning, we think Ze Mean Bean has become the perfect blend of Old and New World.

Hriby Dip

(SERVES 2–4)

We order this creamy Polish mushroom dip every time we visit Ze Mean Bean and fight over who gets to lick the bowl when the dip is gone.

For the mushroom duxelles:

12 ounces button mushrooms, quartered
12 ounces shiitake mushrooms, sliced
½ shallot, chopped
1 tablespoon blended oil
A few tablespoons of white wine
Salt and pepper, to taste

For the dip:

½ onion
1 tablespoon butter
3 ounces mushroom duxelles
3 ounces heavy cream
1 ounce sour cream
Salt and pepper, to taste
2 ounces shredded gruyère cheese
2 pieces pita bread or 1 baguette, sliced
    and lightly toasted

To make the duxelles: In a medium pan, sauté the mushrooms and shallot in the blended oil and deglaze with the white wine. Add salt and pepper and cook for 4–5 minutes until the mushrooms are tender. Remove from the pan.

Reserve 3 ounces to make the dip. The rest may be refrigerated for up to 3 days or frozen for 3 months.

To make the dip: Slice the onion into ½-inch-wide strips and place in a sauté pan with the butter. Cook over medium heat until the onion is soft and golden brown.

Add the duxelles to the pan of onions along with the heavy and sour creams and cook until the liquid is reduced by half and the mixture is thick. Season with salt and pepper to taste.

Stir in the cheese until it melts. Serve with toasted pita or baguette.

Bigos

(SERVES 12)

Traditionally made with cabbage and multiple cuts of meat, including kielbasa, bigos is considered a national dish of Poland. Ze Mean Bean's version uses Polish bacon, which is cooked but not smoked and is less fatty with a milder flavor than American bacon. It can be found at Polish delis, including Krakus, which is next door to the restaurant. One pound of regular slab bacon can be substituted. Vegeta is a bouillon-style seasoning of dried vegetables and spices like black pepper and nutmeg. It can also be purchased at Krakus, and on the Internet. "Whether we are putting our own twist on an old Dornic family recipe or creating a new recipe from scratch, it's most important to us to be true to the traditional ingredients of Eastern Europe."

1 pound pork butt, trimmed and cut into 1-inch chunks

1–2 tablespoons olive oil, or as needed

½ onion, diced

2 carrots, peeled, halved, and sliced

½ clove garlic, chopped fine

½ pound button mushrooms, sliced

½ pound Polish bacon, cubed

3 pounds smoked Polish kielbasa, cut into half moons

1 (16-ounce) can sauerkraut

1 ounce tomato paste

8 ounces canned tomato fillets (seeded and sliced tomato)

2 teaspoons paprika

Vegeta to taste

Salt and pepper, to taste

In a stewpot, heat a few tablespoons of oil and brown the pork butt chunks on all sides. Remove and set aside.

Add the onion, carrots, garlic, and mushrooms to the pot, with a little more oil if it seems dry. Cook them for a few minutes, stirring occasionally, until they start to soften, then add the bacon and sausage.

Once the fat has rendered from the meat and the vegetables are translucent, add the sauerkraut, tomato paste and tomatoes, paprika, reserved pork chunks, and 3½ cups of water.

Season with Vegeta to taste and simmer for 1 hour, stirring often, until the sauce is thickened and the pork is tender. Season with salt and pepper to taste. Serve with warm sourdough bread.

BALTIMORE COUNTY

FLAVOR CUPCAKERY

SCOTTS CORNER SHOPPING CENTER
10253 YORK ROAD
COCKEYSVILLE, MD 21030
(410) 891-8220
FLAVORCUPCAKERY.COM
OWNER: SHELLEY STANNARD

Cupcakes have been the Big Thing for several years now, and there are oodles of bakeries popping up that specialize in the miniature cakes. The Baltimore area has its share, even boasting three cupcake-peddling food trucks that hit the mean streets, dispensing sugary happiness in three-dollar doses. One of those trucks, a chocolate brown van with a blue roof, belongs to Flavor Cupcakery.

We have to admit we've eaten a lot of cupcakes in our day, usually preferring homemade to store-bought, but Flavor's creations are some of our very favorites, ever. Their cakes are moist and the frostings are superbly creamy. And the cupcakes that come from Shelley Stannard's bakery are even fine enough to have won the Food Network's *Cupcake Wars* against some pretty stiff competition. "The *Cupcake Wars* experience was something I'll never forget," says Stannard. "We went into it with a lot of confidence, truly believing we have unique and spectacular cupcakes." And indeed they do. Not merely cupcakes, Flavor's treats are confections. Many have fillings as well as frosting, like the chocolate ganache surprise within the Chocolate Dipped Vanilla Macaroon and the Luscious Lemon's lemon curd center.

While it's most convenient for some of us to wait until the Flavor Cupcakery truck visits our neighborhood, others prefer to visit the bakery in person. In addition to the Cockeysville outpost, there's another one in Bel Air, at 118 North Tollgate Road. These brick-and-mortar shops serve not only cupcakes but also cake pops, truffles, brownies, and macarons. They'll even do wedding cakes. And all are delicious. But don't just take our word for it—try them yourself.

CHOCOLATE ORANGE MARNIER CUPCAKES

(MAKES 24 CUPCAKES)

These chocolate cakes, filled with a chocolate ganache infused with orange and Grand Marnier and topped with vanilla buttercream and chocolate curls, make a fine finish to a great meal.

For the cupcakes:

¼ pound (1 stick) unsalted butter, softened
1½ cups sugar
2 eggs
1 teaspoon vanilla extract
1½ cups all-purpose flour
½ cup baking cocoa
1 teaspoon baking soda
¼ teaspoon salt
½ cup buttermilk
½ cup water

For the Grand Marnier ganache:

8 ounces semisweet chocolate, coarsely chopped
1 cup heavy cream
1 tablespoon unsalted butter, at room temperature
Zest of ½ orange
½ teaspoon orange extract
½ ounce Grand Marnier liqueur

For the vanilla buttercream:

½ pound (2 sticks) unsalted butter, softened
3–4 cups confectioners' sugar, sifted
2–4 tablespoons milk or heavy cream
¼ teaspoon table salt
1 tablespoon vanilla extract

For assembly:

Chocolate curls (see Note)
Orange sanding sugar

To make the cupcakes: Adjust the oven rack to the middle position; preheat oven to 375°F. Line 24 holes of standard muffin/cupcake tins with paper or foil liners.

In a large bowl, cream the butter and sugar until light and fluffy. Add the eggs, one at a time, beating well after each addition. Beat in the vanilla.

In another bowl, combine the flour, cocoa, baking soda, and salt. In a separate bowl, combine the buttermilk and water. Add the dry ingredients to the creamed mixture alternately with buttermilk and water, beating well after each addition.

Fill the paper-lined muffin cups two-thirds full. Bake 15–20 minutes or until a toothpick inserted in the center comes out clean. Cool for 10 minutes before removing from the pans to wire racks to cool completely.

To make the Grand Marnier ganache: Place the chocolate in a medium heatproof bowl; set aside.

Place the cream in a small saucepan over medium heat and bring to a simmer. Pour over the chocolate and let stand until the chocolate has softened, about 5 minutes.

Add the butter, orange zest, and liquids, stirring until smooth. Let cool slightly before using.

To make the vanilla buttercream: Begin with butter that is softened but not melted; the texture should ideally be like ice cream. Beat the butter for a few minutes in a mixer with the paddle attachment on medium speed. Turn the speed to low and add 3 cups of confectioners' sugar. Beat until the sugar and butter have been completely incorporated.

Increase the mixer speed to medium. Add the vanilla extract, salt, and 2 tablespoons of milk or cream and beat for 3 minutes.

If the frosting is too runny, add more sugar. If the frosting needs to be thinned out, add more milk, 1 tablespoon at a time.

To assemble the cupcakes: Using your index finger, poke a hole about ¾-inch deep into the top of each cupcake. Using a piping bag, fill each cupcake with the ganache. Using the same ganache, pipe a ring around the top of the cupcake, leaving a hole in the center. Using a star tip, pipe the vanilla buttercream on top of the cupcake. Sprinkle with chocolate curls and orange sugar.

Note: To make chocolate curls, use a vegetable peeler to scrape curls from a block of room-temperature chocolate.

Havana Road Cuban Cafe

8 W Pennsylvania Avenue
Towson, MD 21204
(410) 494-8222
havanaroad.com
Owner: Chef Marta Quintana

Marta Quintana didn't start out in the restaurant business. After catering her own wedding in 1985, she hung up her apron and spent her days as vice president of sales and marketing for a pharmaceutical distributor. Then the recession hit, her job disappeared, and the Cuban-born Quintana got back into food in a big way. First was Havana Road Artisanal Foods, which started out as a line of salsas and condiments and now includes Freshpak meals like Cuban black beans and rice and ropa vieja. Then Chef Quintana opened her little storefront restaurant, Havana Road Cuban Cafe, in Towson in 2010.

"Restaurants are for the passionate and committed at heart," she says. "It's your life." It is so much a part of Chef Marta's life that she calls her own mother the "executive executive chef" of Havana Road. "Her traditional recipes keep our Cuban menu down

home and true to its roots." Other recipes come from her grandmother's and great-grandmother's neighbors in Cuba, which before the Castro revolution was a "mecca for cultures from all over the world—Asians, Lebanese, Moroccans, Spaniards, African Americans, Jews, Germans." These multicultural influences can be found at Havana Road in weekend specials, which are very popular with the customers.

It's safe to say that all of Quintana's cooking is popular with her customers. "When diners call me out of the kitchen to say, 'We love your food—it's wonderful and fresh,' I feel a great sense of accomplishment." The media, too, love Havana Road, which has received kudos from *Baltimore* magazine, the *Baltimore Business Journal,* and the Restaurant Association of Maryland. Chef Marta takes it in stride. She enjoys the ability to be creative doing something she loves, and "most of all, it's like having a dinner party every day and making people happy with great food!"

ROASTED RED PEPPER & SPICY MANGO GAZPACHO

(SERVES 4–6)

3 tablespoons extra virgin olive oil
1 medium Vidalia onion, diced
1 small green bell pepper, diced
6 garlic cloves, minced
1 teaspoon onion powder
1 teaspoon garlic powder
1 teaspoon ground cumin
Pinch of kosher salt
Pinch of freshly ground black pepper
½ cup dry white wine
5 large roasted red peppers
2 sun-dried tomatoes, chopped
2 plum tomatoes, chopped
1 cup crème fraîche
¾ cup mayonnaise
2½–3 cups vegetable stock
2 ripe mangoes, peeled, pitted, and cut into chunks
1 whole jalapeño
Salt, sugar, and chopped fresh mint for garnish,
    if desired
4–6 chilled martini glasses

In a medium pot over medium heat, combine the olive oil, onion, bell pepper, garlic, onion powder, garlic powder, cumin, and salt and pepper. Cook for 2 minutes. Add the wine. Cook for 3 more minutes or until the onions are translucent. Set aside.

In a food processor, place the roasted red peppers, sun-dried tomatoes, plum tomatoes, crème fraîche, and mayo. Process for 1 minute, then add the onion-pepper mixture and 2½ cups of vegetable stock and process until smooth. If the mixture seems too thick, add more of the stock. Refrigerate.

Puree the mangoes and jalapeño, seeds and all, in a food processor until smooth. Set aside.

If desired, mix salt and sugar in equal parts with finely chopped mint in a small bowl. Dip the chilled martini glasses, upside down, into a shallow bowl of water, then dip the glasses into the sugar-mint mixture. Ladle gazpacho into the glasses and top with a dollop of mango puree.

CARNE CON PAPAS

(SERVES 4–6)

4 tablespoons olive oil

1 onion, chopped

1 small green bell pepper, minced

6 garlic cloves, minced

1 tablespoon tomato paste

½ teaspoon kosher salt

½ teaspoon ground cumin

1 teaspoon dried oregano

1 teaspoon onion powder

2 (8-ounce) cans tomato sauce

½ cup white wine

2 bay leaves

3 tablespoons pimiento-stuffed green olives

2 tablespoons small capers

1 tablespoon diced roasted red pepper

2 pounds lean stewing beef, cubed

5 potatoes, peeled and quartered

Salt and freshly ground black pepper

White rice, for serving

Heat the olive oil over medium heat in a large, deep frying pan with a lid. Add the onion and bell pepper and cook, stirring occasionally, until the onion is translucent, about 4–5 minutes. Stir in the garlic. Add the tomato paste and ½ cup of water and stir until paste and water are incorporated. Then add the salt, cumin, oregano, onion powder, tomato sauce, and wine. Cook for about 5 minutes, stirring constantly. Finally, add the bay leaves, olives, capers, roasted red pepper, and the beef.

Add enough water to the pan (you could use beer, if you'd like) to cover the beef. Bring to a boil, then reduce heat to medium low.

Cover the pan and simmer for 1½–2 hours, until the beef is tender. If the water seems to be evaporating too quickly, add a bit more.

Uncover the pan and add the potatoes. Season the dish with salt and freshly ground pepper. Cover the pan and cook about 20 minutes longer, until the potatoes are fork tender. Reseason with more salt and pepper, if necessary.

Serve over white rice.

Peach Mojito

(SERVES 4–6)

4 large peaches (about 1 pound), unpeeled and chopped
½ cup simple syrup (see Note)
¼ cup fresh lime juice (about 1 lime)
½ cup firmly packed fresh mint leaves
4 cups or 1 liter of club soda, chilled
2½ cups white rum
¼ cup brandy
Fresh mint sprigs, for garnish
Peach wedges, for garnish

Process the peaches, syrup, and lime juice in a blender or food processor until smooth. You should have about 3 cups.

Muddle the mint leaves against the bottom and sides of a glass pitcher to release their flavors.

Add the club soda, rum, brandy, and peach mixture; stir to combine.

Garnish and serve immediately over ice.

Note: To make the simple syrup, combine equal parts water and sugar in a saucepan and boil until the sugar has dissolved. Allow to cool completely before using. Keeps indefinitely in a covered container in the refrigerator.

LINWOOD'S

25 CROSSROADS DRIVE
OWINGS MILLS, MD 21117
(410) 356-3030
LINWOODS.COM
OWNERS: CHEF LINWOOD DAME, ELLEN DAME
EXECUTIVE CHEF: TOM DEVINE

After graduating from the Culinary Institute of America in Hyde Park, New York, Linwood Dame took a job as the executive chef at a French bistro in Richmond, Virginia called the Butlery. During his tenure in Virginia, he and his wife, Ellen, spoke often of opening their own restaurant, a tiny place with Ellen working the front of the house and Linwood behind

the stove. They'd visit Baltimore occasionally and felt that the area could use a restaurant that would bring some fresh, West Coast ideas to the restaurant-conservative town. They found a spot in the up-and-coming burb of Owings Mills, which back in the '80s was still somewhat undeveloped. Today, twenty-five years later, Linwood's is still going strong.

Linwood's is bit larger than the tiny place Linwood and Ellen first envisioned. With an open kitchen and contemporary decor that received a touch-up a handful of years back, the restaurant would not look out of place in Manhattan or Los Angeles. The food is New American with some fusion twists, like the char siu glaze on an appetizer of baby back ribs or the charmoula vinaigrette on a Mediterranean-style salad, but most of it is straightforward and uncomplicated. As Chef Dame says, "Complicated ingredients don't always make the best cuisine. Sometimes the simplest things are the finest. Then it becomes a discipline of preparing the dishes correctly and consistently."

Linwood's executive chef is Tom Devine, who has been with Dame since the Butlery days. A graduate of Johnson & Wales University, Devine, like Dame, is a stickler for quality. His credo is "Use only the best seasonal ingredients prepared with proven cooking techniques." And while he feels it's fun to create new dishes and push the boundaries, "in the end, I want guests to have an enjoyable experience when eating my food." Some of the most enjoyable food that comes out of Devine's kitchen includes the tender espresso-rubbed rib eye, a fine broiled crab cake that can compete with the best around, and the best-selling butter-poached lobster. Linwood's also has pizzas, made in their wood-burning oven, and a fine burger, so diners can just as easily eat frugally as go whole hog.

"Being a chef is hard work with long hours, but if you truly enjoy cooking and entertaining people, it is well worth the effort," says Devine.

CHILLED LOBSTER SALAD
WITH LEMON THYME MADELEINE

(SERVES 4)

For the herbed vinaigrette:

2 ounces mint
2 ounces cilantro
2 ounces basil
2 ounces dill
2 eggs
1 ounce grated Parmigiano Reggiano cheese
¼ cup lemon juice
2 cups extra virgin olive oil

For the lemon thyme madeleines:

3 ounces unsalted butter
⅔ cup powdered sugar
½ cup flour
¼ cup ground almonds
½ cup egg whites
1 ounce chopped thyme
Zest of 2 lemons

For the lobster and salad:

2 (1½-pound) lobsters, cooked and cooled
Herbed vinaigrette
1 head hydroponic bibb lettuce
12 slices avocado
16 segments red grapefruit
8 lemon thyme madeleines

To make the herbed vinaigrette: Blanch all the herbs in boiling salted water for 5 seconds, shock in ice cold water. and chop.

Place the eggs, cheese, and lemon juice in a blender on medium speed. Slowly add the oil in a steady stream to emulsify the vinaigrette. Strain through a fine mesh strainer. Chill.

To make the lemon thyme madeleines: Preheat oven to 350°F.

In a small saucepan, melt the butter over medium heat and cook until nutty and brown but not burned. Set aside to cool.

Sift together the powdered sugar and flour, then stir in the ground almonds. Whisk the egg whites until frothy. Stir in the almond mixture until thoroughly combined. Add the brown butter, thyme, and lemon zest.

Spoon batter into a greased madeleine pan. Bake for 5 minutes, until golden brown. Flip out of the pan while still warm.

To make the lobster and salad: Remove the lobster meat from the shells. Chop the tail and knuckle meat; reserve the claws. Toss the chopped lobster meat with herbed vinaigrette to coat lightly. Season with salt.

Lay out two leaves of bibb lettuce in the center of each plate. Top with lobster salad. Arrange avocado and grapefruit segments on the outside edge of the lettuce leaves. Garnish with lobster claws and two warm madeleines.

Grilled Rockfish with Mango Pineapple Salsa

(SERVES 4)

1½ cups diced plum tomato
1½ cups diced pineapple
1½ cups diced mango
½ cup diced red onion
2 tablespoons chopped cilantro
2 teaspoons seeded and chopped jalapeño
3 tablespoons lime juice
3 tablespoons orange juice
½ cup chopped macadamia nuts
Salt and pepper
2 tablespoons olive oil
4 (6-ounce) rockfish fillets

Combine the tomato, pineapple, mango, onion, cilantro, jalapeño, lime juice, orange juice, and macadamias in a bowl. Season to taste with salt and pepper and set aside for at least 1 hour to allow flavors to meld.

Preheat the grill to medium-hot.

Rub the rockfish with olive oil and season with salt and pepper. Grill each side of the rockfish for 5 minutes, until done, flipping only once.

Spoon salsa over each fillet and serve.

McFaul's IronHorse Tavern

At Sanders' Corner
2260 Cromwell Bridge Road
Parkville, MD 21234
(410) 828-1625
McFaulsironhorsetavern.com
Owners: Glen McFaul, Kristin
McFaul, Walt Lashno,
Mat Remsnyder, Chuck Trunk
Chef: Evan Orser

The original Sanders' Corner started out life as a blacksmith shop in the late 1800s, and a post office after that. In the 1950s the Sanders family turned the place into a general store cum ice cream and sandwich shop and later a family restaurant. Today the wide, shady porch and view of the Loch Raven reservoir still lure diners into the restaurant's current incarnation, McFaul's IronHorse Tavern. The "iron horse" in the name is both a reference to the Ma & Pa Railroad that ran nearby and a "tribute to Baltimore's iron horses—legends like Oriole Cal Ripken Jr. and Colt John Unitas," says owner Glen McFaul. McFaul himself is a grandson of one of Baltimore's true iron horses, Orioles Hall of Fame umpire attendant Ernie Tyler, who worked 3,769 consecutive Os home games—besting Ripken's record by more than a thousand games.

McFaul's caters to a wide clientele—older folks for lunch, the younger crowd for live music, Ravens fans for game day—so the menu offers a little bit of everything. There are hearty sandwiches and comfort food entrees alongside more sophisticated dishes like bison carpaccio crostini and a deconstructed sushi roll.

McFaul's chef Evan Orser is a graduate of the Pennsylvania Institute of Culinary Arts in Pittsburgh. He spent time at Peerce's Plantation (now the Grille at Peerce's), Josef's Country Inn in Fallston, and Looney's in Bel Air before ending up at McFaul's. A self-described "adrenaline junkie," Orser loves the fast pace and pressure of working in a professional kitchen. "Just being in there makes me happy." Much of the food he serves is sourced from Maryland purveyors, from Gunpowder Bison and Albright Farms beef and turkey to Tilghman Island seafood. "Fresh and local—can't beat that," says Chef Orser.

When asked about his favorite things to cook, Orser laughs. "That's like asking a banker what bill he likes to count the most." He continued, "I was trained by old-school chefs, so I tend to take an old-school approach to cooking, taking simple foods and transforming them into something mouthwatering." The mouthwatering cuisine he produces at McFaul's includes a macaroni and cheese gilded with lobster chunks and a sweet and spicy teriyaki salmon dish, the first of which is featured here.

LOBSTER MAC & CHEESE

(SERVES 2–3)

⅓ cup lobster stock

1⅛ cups heavy cream

4 ounces fresh Maine lobster, diced

Salt and pepper, to taste

1½ cups grated cheddar jack cheese

½ cup grated gruyère cheese

½ cup grated Parmesan cheese

2 cups cooked pasta shells

½ cup seasoned bread crumbs

Preheat oven to 350°F.

Pour the lobster stock into a saucepan. Reduce to one-quarter of its original volume over medium heat. Add the heavy cream and reduce more. Add the cheeses and stir. Add the lobster pieces and salt and pepper to taste.

Combine the cooked pasta with the cheese-lobster sauce in an oven-safe dish. Top with bread crumbs and bake until golden brown, approximately 5–8 minutes.

THE MILTON INN

14833 YORK ROAD
SPARKS, MD 21152
(410) 771-4366
MILTONINN.COM
OWNER: CHEF BRIAN BOSTON

The quaint fieldstone building known as the Milton Inn has had quite a history since it was built in 1740. At times it was a private residence, for a while it was a boys' school known as the Milton Academy (with John Wilkes Booth its most notorious alumnus), and since 1947 it's been one of the most esteemed restaurants in Baltimore County. Originally designed to be a home, the restaurant utilizes six different rooms as the front of the house, each decorated in a colonial style. The effect is both formal and intimate, the perfect setting for a quiet dinner for two or an elegant dinner party.

The Milton Inn's executive chef, Brian Boston, is a graduate of the esteemed Culinary Institute of America. He started his career as a line cook at Peerce's Plantation, now the Grille at Peerce's, before taking over the Milton Inn in 1997. His menu showcases contemporary American fare with a French twist, and a few traditional Maryland dishes as well.

Named Chef of the Year for 2011 by the Restaurant Association of Maryland, Chef Boston is a strong proponent of the farm-to-table movement and is fond of utilizing the seafood so identifiable with the Chesapeake Bay region, as in his award-winning Maryland crab soup. "We use a lot of local ingredients," he said. "We have high-quality meats, fish, and produce. We do our own butchering, and our pastries are made in-house." Little wonder the Milton Inn received the DiRoNA Award (Distinguished Restaurants of North America), the only Baltimore County restaurant to achieve this honor, and the Star Diamond award from the American Academy of Hospitality Sciences.

The chef is not one to rest on his laurels. For some time now he's been working on a new restaurant in Howard County called the Highland Inn, which will bring a much-needed full-service restaurant to the community of Highland, Maryland. Rest assured, however, he will remain in the kitchen at the Milton Inn, continuing to please with dishes like his roasted duck with pear gastrique and his bacon-enriched oyster stew.

MILTON INN OYSTER STEW

(SERVES 15)

"Salinity is important to this dish; it should be pleasantly salty. You can also change this recipe to your taste, substituting curry powder for the Old Bay or tarragon for the parsley."

½ pound unsalted butter

6 slices bacon, cooked and crumbled, fat reserved

1 cup minced onion

1 cup minced celery

3 tablespoons flour

3 tablespoons Old Bay seasoning

2 quarts cold half-and-half

1 quart oysters with their liquor

1 tablespoon Worcestershire sauce

Salt, to taste

1 teaspoon black pepper

Finely chopped parsley

Melt the butter in a heavy-bottomed pot along with the reserved bacon fat. Add the onions and celery and sweat the vegetables over medium heat until soft.

Add the flour and Old Bay and stir well to form a roux. Cook for 1 minute.

Add the half-and-half, whisking well to prevent lumps.

Add the oyster liquor and Worcestershire and simmer for 10 minutes. Add salt and pepper to taste.

Add the oysters at the last minute, just to heat through. Be careful not to overcook.

Serve in bowls, garnished with crumbled bacon and chopped parsley.

ORCHARD MARKET & CAFE

8815 ORCHARD TREE LANE
BALTIMORE, MD 21286
(410) 339-7700
ORCHARDMARKETANDCAFE.COM
OWNERS: JASON BULKELEY, SHARAREH BULKELEY
CHEF: NAHID VAEZPOUR

Back in 1988, Michael Mir opened the Orchard Market & Cafe as a coffee shop and gourmet food market specializing in Mediterranean and Middle Eastern foods. It didn't become a full-service Persian restaurant until a couple of years later, after he hired Chef Nahid Vaezpour, a recent immigrant from Iran and a widowed mother of eighteen children.

Vaezpour's experience with cooking for a large number of people served her well in the restaurant kitchen. While her specialty is home-style comfort food, Vaezpour's most popular dish is the chicken *fesenjune*, a *khoresh* or stew with a complex sweet-and-sour tomato-based sauce flavored with pomegranate molasses, ground walnuts, cinnamon, and cardamom. The chef also prepares some even fancier special occasion foods, like

the elaborate *shirin polo,* a chicken dish traditionally served at weddings and other festive events. Current Orchard Market owner Jason Bulkeley calls the dish "a visual delight" of jeweled saffron rice with barberries, raisins, almonds, and shredded carrots.

Bulkeley, a former Orchard Market waiter, and his Persian-born wife Sharareh bought the restaurant from Mir in 1997. And while the kitchen is still firmly under the direction of Chef Vaezpour, Bulkeley likes to play with traditional Persian flavors and invent some Persian-fusion dishes of his own. The Spicy Pistachio Chicken recipe is one example.

When asked why Orchard Market has remained popular for so many years, Bulkeley has this to say: "Our customers like us because we're different, we're not a chain. We've created a niche that no one can duplicate." He estimates that 90 percent of his customers are regulars; one couple has visited multiple times a week for fifteen years. It's clear that diners at the Orchard Market are treated like family.

Spicy Pistachio Chicken

(SERVES 2–4)

2 tablespoons vegetable oil

1 cup chopped onion

1 pound boneless, skinless chicken breast, cut into strips

½ cup shelled whole unsalted pistachios

½ pound crimini mushrooms

1 can artichoke hearts, drained and cut in half

1 cup fresh chicken stock

½ cup tomato puree

3 tablespoons Madras curry powder

Pinch of cayenne pepper, or to taste

2–4 cloves garlic, chopped

Pinch each of dried cilantro, parsley, and fenugreek

½ cup finely ground pistachios, plus more for garnish

½ cup sour cream

Salt and pepper, to taste

3 tablespoons finely minced parsley

3 cups cooked basmati rice, for serving

Heat the vegetable oil in a large sauté pan over medium heat. Add the onions and a pinch of salt and cook until softened, stirring occasionally, about 5 minutes.

Add the chicken breast strips and turn up the heat to medium-high. Stir-fry the chicken until it's about half cooked, then add the whole pistachios, the mushrooms, and the artichoke hearts.

Add the chicken stock, tomato puree, curry powder, cayenne, garlic, and herbs to the pan. Bring to a boil, then turn down the heat. Let the mixture simmer until the chicken is completely cooked through, about 10 minutes.

Whisk in ½ cup of the ground pistachios and the sour cream to thicken the sauce. Taste for seasoning and add salt and pepper and the minced parsley. Serve over basmati rice, and finish with a sprinkling of ground pistachios.

EGGPLANT & ARTICHOKE APPETIZER

(SERVES 4–6)

This dish is one of the most popular items at Orchard Market & Cafe.

1 large Italian eggplant

Salt

¼ cup vegetable oil

3 cans artichoke hearts, drained

1 cup sour cream

1 cup honey Dijon mustard, preferably
   Grey Poupon

2 teaspoons minced fresh dill

4–5 tablespoons pomegranate molasses

6 ounces Bulgarian feta

¼ cup pitted black olives

Pita bread triangles for serving

Peel the eggplant. Cut off and discard the ends. Cut the eggplant in half and slice into strips about 6 x 3 x ½ inches. Salt the eggplant strips well and lay them flat on paper towels for at least ½ hour and up to 1½ hours.

When ready to cook, rinse the eggplant under cold water to remove excess salt. Blot dry.

Gently fry the eggplant in the vegetable oil until tender. Remove from the oil and drain well on paper-towel-lined plates, changing the towels at least once.

Place the eggplant strips in a 9 x 13-inch baking dish. Arrange the artichoke hearts over the eggplant.

Preheat oven to 375°F.

In a bowl, combine the sour cream, mustard, dill, and pomegranate molasses into a thick sauce. If the sauce seems a bit runny, add a little more sour cream.

Crumble the feta over the eggplant and artichokes. Pour the sauce over all. Top with black olives.

Bake for 15–20 minutes until hot; the cheese and sauce will begin to brown.

Remove portions from the pan with a spatula, trying to preserve the integrity of the layers. Surround with pita triangles, pointed ends out.

Gruyère Crusted Salmon
with Fingerling Potatoes, Haricots Verts
& Soy Citrus Glaze

(SERVES 2)

For the potatoes and haricots verts:

4 ounces haricots verts, trimmed
6 ounces fingerling potatoes, cut in half on the bias
1 teaspoon minced fresh rosemary
½ teaspoon Lawry's seasoning salt
1 tablespoon blended oil

For the soy citrus glaze:

2 tablespoons soy sauce
2 tablespoons honey
1 tablespoon Dijon mustard
4 tablespoons lemon juice
8 tablespoons blended oil

For the salmon:

½ cup panko or unseasoned bread crumbs
¼ pound grated gruyère cheese
1 tablespoon finely chopped parsley
½ teaspoon salt
¼ teaspoon pepper
2 (8-ounce) Atlantic salmon fillets
1 ounce yellow mustard
½ ounce prepared horseradish
1 tablespoon olive oil oil for cooking
Minced chives or scallions, for garnish

To make the potatoes and haricots verts: Preheat oven to 350°F.

Bring a pot of water to a boil and add the beans. Boil for about 1½ minutes or until they become brighter green and slightly tender. Drain and season with a small amount of salt and pepper.

Toss the remaining ingredients together and roast, uncovered, in the preheated oven for 20–25 minutes or until the potatoes are tender.

To make the soy citrus glaze: Place the first four ingredients in a food processor and blend until fully incorporated. Once mixed, slowly drizzle in the oil and process until completely combined.

To make the salmon: Place the bread crumbs, gruyère, parsley, salt, and pepper in a food processor and blend thoroughly. Evenly coat the tops of the salmon fillets with the yellow mustard and horseradish, then pat on an even layer of the gruyère bread crumbs.

Heat an ovenproof sauté pan over medium heat and add a tablespoon or so of oil. Once the pan is hot, place the fish, crust side down, in the pan. Set the pan in the preheated oven and cook for 8–10 minutes.

To serve: Reheat haricots verts in a small skillet. Arrange half of the beans and potatoes on each of two plates. Place one salmon fillet on top. Using a spoon, drizzle the sauce over the salmon. Garnish with minced chives or scallions.

OUTSIDE
BALTIMORE

Antrim 1844

30 Trevanion Road
Taneytown, MD 21787
(410) 756-6812
antrim1844.com
Owners: Richard Mollett, Dorothy Mollett
Chef: Spencer Wolff

Once a plantation, the Antrim 1844 Country House Hotel still reflects the gracious style of the mid-1800s. Carefully restored by owners Richard and Dorothy Mollett, the elegant twenty-four-acre estate in the Catoctin Mountains is often thought of as an ideal location for a romantic getaway, wedding, or corporate meeting, but Antrim 1844 also serves a sumptuous six-course prix-fixe menu seven days a week.

The meal always begins with cocktails and hors d'oeuvres. Diners can stroll the beautifully landscaped grounds during the summer or, in the winter, relax by the fireplace in the drawing room. The Smokehouse Restaurant is a bit more austere than the lavishly decorated rooms in the Mansion, with a brick floor, dark wood, and paintings of nineteenth-century military heroes on the walls.

The chef at Antrim is Cordon Bleu–educated Spencer Wolff, who most recently was the executive chef at the Hyatt Regency Schaumburg-Chicago and who has worked with some of the world's top chefs, such as Charlie Trotter, Gordon Sinclair, and Stéphane Tournier at Château de Brindos in Biarritz, France. But his real culinary education started at home. "In the summers I'd fish with my father and in the fall we'd hunt, and we ate what we caught. My mother was a fantastic cook and baker. [She made] amazing breads and pastries, while my father did the artisan work—sausage and charcuterie. I suppose watching them develop dishes with limited resources was my initiation to becoming a chef. The most satisfying aspects of this profession

and what keeps me motivated are its endless possibilities and the immediate gratification of producing a quality dish."

Chef Wolff is a big proponent of seasonal cooking, not only with ingredients but techniques. "In spring and summer there are all the wonderful vegetables, especially tomatoes. I love tomatoes. In the fall and winter I love braising and stews . . . short ribs, pork belly, lamb tagine, cassoulet. And the abundance of game and assorted squashes is amazing!"

The menu at Antrim is constantly changing, so even popular items get pushed aside for new dishes. "We're constantly changing and working to source the best product to put on our plates."

Butternut Squash Soup
with Butter Poached Lobster
& Tahitian Vanilla

(SERVES 4)

For the soup:

2 butternut squash
2–3 tablespoons vegetable oil (divided)
2 tablespoons sugar
½ Tahitian vanilla bean, split and scraped
8 ounces heavy cream
8 ounces vegetable stock
Salt and white pepper

For the lobster:

1 (1-pound) lobster
1 pound butter, melted
Salt and white pepper

To make the soup: Preheat oven to 350°F.

Peel and seed one squash and cut it into small dice. Reserve the dice.

Halve the unpeeled squash lengthwise, place the halves cut side down on a baking sheet, and lightly oil the skin. Roast for approximately 30 minutes, or until the skin begins to bubble. Remove from the oven. When cool enough to work with, remove and discard the seeds and skin.

In a heavy-bottomed saucepan, heat 1 tablespoon of the oil, add the baked squash, and sauté over medium heat. While it begins to release its water, continue to stir, allowing the squash to lightly caramelize. Add the sugar and vanilla bean, followed by the heavy cream and vegetable stock. Simmer for about 20 minutes.

If it becomes too thick, add additional stock or even a small amount of water.

Remove from the heat and remove the vanilla bean. Puree the squash in a blender, starting on low speed and gradually increasing to high. Blend for about 45 seconds on high and remove. Adjust the seasoning with salt and pepper. The soup should have a pronounced scent and flavor of vanilla and be slightly but not overly sweet. Reserve and keep hot.

In a heavy-bottomed sauté pan, preferably nonstick, add enough oil to coat the bottom of the pan. Over medium heat, gently sauté the diced squash until soft. Season and reserve for garnish.

To make the lobster: Prepare an ice bath large enough to submerge the cooked lobster.

In a stockpot bring 4 quarts of water to a boil. Plunge the lobster in headfirst and cook for 3 minutes. Remove and immediately submerge in the ice bath.

When the lobster has cooled, remove the head and claws. Slit the underside of the tail and remove the meat in one piece. Gently crack the claws to remove their meat in one piece. Be sure to feel for the cartilage; this also needs to be removed if present. Continue by removing the knuckle meat. Rinse all the lobster meat under cold water to remove any white residue. Check the tail for veins, and remove them if present. Reserve all the lobster meat in a cold place until ready to proceed.

Season the melted butter with salt and white pepper. Heat the butter to 160°F, but no more or you'll overcook the meat. Use a thermometer to maintain the correct temperature. Slice the tail into four medallions and place them, along with the knuckle and claw meat, in the butter. Gently poach for 7–10 minutes or until heated through. Remove and drain on paper towel.

To assemble: In a pan, reheat the diced squash with some lobster meat. Check and adjust the seasoning.

In the center of each of four bowls, place a small spoonful of diced squash and lobster meat, followed by a lobster medallion. Gently pour the soup around the lobster garnish without covering it.

BALDWIN'S STATION

7618 MAIN STREET
SYKESVILLE, MD 21784
(410) 795-1041
BALDWINSSTATION.COM
OWNER: STEWART DEARIE
CHEF: DUSTIN HEFLIN

One of the most historic buildings in the charming town of Sykesville is a restored train station situated on the Old Main Line of the B&O Railroad. Built in 1883, the Queen Anne–style structure boasts original stained glass windows, a wraparound deck, and twenty-foot ceilings. It's home to an eatery that was awarded the title Favorite Restaurant 2012 by the Restaurant Association of Maryland.

Baldwin's Station, named after the architect who designed the building, offers contemporary cuisine in a historical setting. In the kitchen is Chef Dustin Heflin. "He is full of new, fresh ideas," says the restaurant's owner, Stewart Dearie, an industry veteran who once managed the vaunted and much-missed Conservatory at the Peabody Court Hotel in Baltimore. "Our customers have been raving about his innovative combinations."

Heflin started his cooking career at Baldwin's Station, believe it or not, when he was in high school. A decade later, after earning several degrees in culinary school, he returned to the kitchen where he first fell in love with the restaurant industry. "I jumped at the opportunity to 'come home' to where my career began."

Chef Heflin believes that food brings people and cultures together, and enjoys adding a fusion twist to classic dishes. He may take a traditionally French dish, for example, and put a Spanish or Asian twist on it, depending on how he's feeling that day. He's also a fan of using high-quality, locally sourced, organic produce and meats, and is not averse to playing with more unusual ingredients that diners may not be familiar with. "I love when I can turn skeptics into believers when I take an ingredient, prepare it in a new way, and actually change their outlook on that food. That is when I feel that I have done my job properly."

SAMBUCA MUSSELS WITH ROASTED GARLIC TOAST

(SERVES 1)

10 mussels
1 tablespoon olive oil
1 teaspoon minced garlic
1 teaspoon minced shallot
2½ ounces Sambuca
4 ounces heavy cream
Pinch of minced parsley
Salt and pepper, to taste
1 baguette
4 cloves roasted garlic
8 ounces butter, softened

Wash and clean the mussels; pat dry with paper towels.

In a medium sauté pan, heat the olive oil and cook the mussels until they just start to open, about 4 minutes. Add the garlic and shallot and cook for 1 minute or just until the shallot is translucent.

Remove the pan from the heat and add the Sambuca. Place back on the heat and cook over high heat until the liquid is reduced by half. Add the cream and reduce again by half or until all of the mussels are open, 3–5 minutes. Add parsley and season with salt and pepper to taste.

For the toast, cut the baguette on the bias into ¼-inch-thick slices. Combine the roasted garlic and butter in the bowl of a food processor. Rub a light layer of butter on the baguette slices and broil until the butter melts and the bread is toasted and golden brown, about 2–3 minutes.

Place the mussels in a bowl, pour the juices over, and top with one or two pieces of toast.

CRUSH KITCHEN & WINEHOUSE

114 WEST STREET
ANNAPOLIS, MD 21401
(410) 216-9444
CRUSHWINEHOUSE.COM
OWNERS: BOB LAGGINI, JANET BESANCENEY
CHEF: MICHAEL MORRONE
PASTRY CHEF: NICOLE BOSLEY

Back in 1908, the handsome Italianate building that houses Crush Kitchen & Winehouse started life as the Rescue-Hose Company, aka the local firehouse. Today it's Annapolis's first and only European-style wine bar. The garage doors for the fire engines have been

replaced with windows that provide a scenic view of West Street. The interior is as sleek and modern as the outside is historic, with rich burgundy walls and simple, unadorned furniture.

Crush's executive chef is Michael Morrone, who has cooked in New Mexico as well as in other restaurants in the Annapolis area like Galway Bay Irish Pub and Reynolds Tavern. The chef is a proponent of home-style cooking using local ingredients prepared simply, but with a modern spin. "I concentrate on accentuating the natural flavors of quality ingredients."

Chef Morrone's menu is geared to complement Crush's wide array of libations, which include beers and cocktails as well as a selection of wines. The list of starters and salads is extensive—from prosciutto-wrapped dates to alligator sausage to a salmon salad with ginger soy dressing. There's also cheese and cured meats to be enjoyed with your tasty adult beverage. If you are looking for something more substantial, the entrees are hearty comfort food including rib eye, meat loaf, and roasted duck. And if you prefer to have something sweet with your drink, or are fond of having dessert after dinner, there's bound to be at least one of pastry chef Nicole Bosley's sugary delectables that will catch your eye.

Previously at DC's Panache and Slate Wine Bar, Chef Bosley became the official pastry chef in her house when she was ten, after baking a particularly successful batch of biscuits. She even had to make her own birthday cakes. Though she attended law school, baking was a profession that "would be more relaxing and present more immediate and tangible rewards." Our idea of "tangible rewards" would be one of Chef Bosley's desserts, all made fresh daily.

PORK MEDALLIONS WITH BLACK PEPPER GRAVY

(SERVES 3)

1 pork tenderloin, about 1 pound
Salt and pepper
13 strips applewood-smoked bacon (divided)
1 red bell pepper
½ cup sliced mushrooms
1 teaspoon freshly ground black pepper
½ tablespoon flour
½ cup heavy cream

Preheat oven to 350°F.

Remove the silver skin from the pork tenderloin and split the tenderloin lengthwise to make one wide, flattish piece of meat.

Pound with a meat tenderizing mallet until the meat is about 1 inch thick. Salt and pepper the pork and roll it up, jelly roll style. Wrap the pork roll in ten of the bacon slices, place in a roasting pan, and bake for about 30 minutes, or until the internal temperature reaches 145°F.

Meanwhile, roast the red pepper over a gas flame or on a grill until the skin is blackened and charred. Place in a bowl and cover with plastic wrap. When cool enough to handle, rub off the skin. Core the pepper and cut it into strips. Set aside.

When the pork is done, remove from the oven and allow to rest for 5–10 minutes.

While the pork is resting, cook the remaining three slices of bacon until the fat is rendered and the bacon is crisp. Remove the bacon and set aside for another use. (Or eat it—cook's treat.)

Add the mushrooms to the bacon fat in the pan and cook over medium-high heat until browned. Add the teaspoon of freshly ground black pepper and the flour, whisking well and making sure there are no lumps. Cook for 2 minutes. Add the cream and simmer the sauce until thick.

Slice the pork into 1½-inch-thick medallions. Top with mushroom sauce and strips of roasted bell pepper.

PEACH CRISP WITH MARSHMALLOW ICE CREAM

(SERVES 8)

For the marshmallow ice cream:

2 cups half-and-half
10 ounces marshmallows
2 cups heavy cream
2 teaspoons vanilla extract

For the peach crisp:

2–3 pounds peaches (about 12–14)
1 pint blueberries
1½ cups oatmeal
1½ cups flour
1 cup firmly packed brown sugar
⅔ cup pecans
Pinch of salt
8 tablespoons melted unsalted butter

To make the marshmallow ice cream: Combine the half-and-half and marshmallows in a large pot. Cook over medium-low heat until the marshmallows melt. Remove from heat and refrigerate until cold.

Whip the heavy cream with the vanilla until soft peaks form. Fold in the chilled marshmallow mixture.

Freeze in an ice cream machine according to manufacturer's instructions, typically 20–25 minutes.

To make the peach crisp: Preheat oven to 350°F.

Peel and slice the peaches, then toss them with the blueberries. Put the fruit into a 9 x 13-inch baking pan.

In a separate bowl, combine the oatmeal, flour, brown sugar, pecans, and salt. Drizzle in the melted butter and mix well.

Sprinkle topping over peaches and blueberries. Bake for 35–40 minutes or until browned and crisp on top. Serve with marshmallow ice cream.

While there's no shortage of excellent restaurants in the Baltimore Metro area, other Maryland regions boast some pretty fine dining options as well. The Eastern Shore, just over the Chesapeake Bay Bridge from Anne Arundel County, is a popular destination for both day-trippers and vacationers, and of course is the year-round home to nearly half a million Marylanders.

The Narrows, about seven miles east of the bridge in Grasonville, boasts award-winning crab cakes and cream of crab soup. The restaurant, which sits on the foundation of an old oyster shucking house, offers classic Maryland seafood items like the aforementioned crab dishes, plus a few twists on old favorites. Take the fried oyster Caesar, for example, or the crab and artichoke dip subtly flavored with country ham.

In scenic St. Michael's, due south of Grasonville if one chooses to swim or travel by boat but otherwise a fifty-mile drive, there's the Inn at Perry Cabin. The original inn, named for War of 1812 hero Commodore Oliver Hazard Perry, was built in 1816 and served as the private residence of Samuel Hamilton, Perry's aide-de-camp. Over the many years since, the property served other purposes as a farm and riding camp before being converted to a small hotel in 1980 by the Meyerhoff family of St. Michael's. Later it was purchased by Bernard Ashley, husband of renowned Welsh fashion designer Laura Ashley, who greatly expanded the inn. The now forty-one-room luxury hotel has played host to both celebrities and heads of state and boasts one of only three Maryland restaurants to be awarded the prestigious Four Diamonds by AAA.

The inn's star restaurant, Sherwood's Landing, under the guidance of Executive Chef Daniel Pochron, serves breakfast, lunch, and luxurious dinners to both hotel guests and visitors to the serene Talbot County town.

On the way to St. Michael's, one passes through the town of Easton. There the Bartlett Pear Inn is a popular spot. Easton native Chef Jordan Lloyd and his wife, Alice, run the pear-themed hotel and hope to eventually own the premier restaurant on the Eastern Shore. The Pear is well on its way, offering dishes made with locally sourced Eastern Shore ingredients like vegetables from Emily's Produce, cheeses from Chapel's Country Creamery, and charcuterie from Black Bottom Farm.

ELKRIDGE FURNACE INN

5745 FURNACE AVENUE
ELKRIDGE, MD 21075
(410) 379-9336
ELKRIDGEFURNACEINN.COM
OWNER: CHEF DANIEL WECKER

While trendy bistros in bustling city neighborhoods offer an exciting dining experience, sometimes it's nice to lose oneself in the fantasy of dining in a stately manor home harkening back to a more genteel time. Such is the effect felt while passing through the Federal/Greek Revival entrance of the Elkridge Furnace Inn. The property originally held a tavern in 1744, and an iron smelting furnace was built on the premises in 1750, hence the name. The actual inn was added by James and Andrew Ellicott in the early 1800s.

After some years the property fell into a serious state of disrepair. Persuading the state to lease them the neglected property in the late 1980s, Dan Wecker and his brother Steve refurbished the Inn, which Dan used for his catering business. In 1994 he opened it as a full-scale restaurant. The inn is currently a family-run business, with Dan's wife Donna and children Cameron and Matthias taking on responsibilities from personnel to

groundskeeping, and daughter Genelle acting as executive pastry chef.

While growing up in Lancaster County, Dan Wecker regularly helped out on a small family farm that grew produce and raised livestock. He started cooking at the age of fourteen, when he ran the concession stand at an ice rink. Later, after bouncing around the world as a foreign exchange student, he picked up classic French technique during an apprenticeship with a chef from Grenoble. These experiences helped formulate his philosophy: "Work with classic principles, learn to work with the tools you have, be as fresh and as seasonal as possible, never stop thinking, and love what you are doing."

One of the many skills Dan picked up during his training was whole-animal butchery, and he has passed on those techniques to the young chefs that work under him. At the Elkridge Furnace Inn, they regularly utilize whole hogs and veal calves, producing their own house-made sausages with the off-cuts.

While the menu at the Elkridge Furnace Inn reflects this French culinary background, there is a clear nod to local favorites like crab cakes and crab dip.

CRAB DIP TWO WAYS

(SERVES 12)

Both versions can be served with crackers, French bread rounds, and/or crudités. They also work well as fillings for mini tart shells and mushroom caps, as sandwich spreads, or as toppings for pizza or crostini.

For serving cold:

1 pint mayonnaise
¼ cup lemon juice
2 tablespoons Worcestershire sauce
¼ cup capers
1 tablespoon Cajun spice
2 teaspoons hot sauce
1 pound gruyère cheese, shredded
1 pound jumbo lump crabmeat

For serving warm:

½ pint sour cream
1 (8-ounce) package cream cheese, softened
¼ cup lemon juice
2 tablespoons Worcestershire sauce
¼ cup capers
1 tablespoon Cajun spice
2 teaspoons hot sauce
1 pound gruyère cheese, shredded
1 pound jumbo lump crabmeat

To serve cold: Place everything but the crabmeat in a bowl, stirring well to combine. Gently fold in the crabmeat.

To serve warm: Preheat oven to 350°F.

Place everything but the crabmeat in a bowl, stirring well to combine. Gently fold in the crabmeat. Transfer the mixture to an ovenproof pan and heat for 15 minutes.

Factor's Row

26 Market Space
Annapolis, MD 21401
(410) 280-8686
FACTORSROW.COM
Owner: Bruce Gardner
Chef: Keith Long

In keeping with the scenic harbor location and the steady stream of tourists who flock to said location, Annapolis is amply populated with seafood restaurants serving traditional crab cakes, crab imperial, and oysters on the half shell. The dining scene in this town is pretty conservative, but some people, like Factor's Row chef Keith Long, feel that Annapolis is inching toward more food-forward restaurants.

Factor's Row is one of them. A quick glance at the menu will assure a passing tourist

that it too offers a nice selection of fish and crab dishes. But there's something remarkable going on here. Chef Long's playful use of disparate flavors and textures is bold and exciting. Sure, many restaurants offer grilled fish, but here it's mahimahi combined with golden raisins, pomegranate molasses, and crispy brussels sprouts. Want some sliders? How about lamb sliders with goat cheese and gremolata? And if you want popcorn for a snack, here's some duck fat to warm your soul.

"I am passionate about searching out perfect, often unusual ingredients and combining them in surprising ways to create simple, clean, and big flavors," says the chef, who was born in Texas but raised in Annapolis. He worked on the Eastern Shore for a bit before coming on board at Factor's Row. The lifelong exposure to the bounty of the Chesapeake Bay has made seafood his favorite thing to cook. "I love the history behind dishes, and while honoring the past I like to put in my own twist to make something familiar yet unexpected." This is true of his crab cakes. While quite straightforward, they are given a southern twist by setting them in a bed of grits, with fried green tomatoes and pickled watermelon rind on the side.

One of the most popular dishes at Factor's Row is the scallops, which are beautifully simple but have big flavor. The dish, with its combination

of greens and vivid yellows, also packs a visual punch. And that lamb slider is Chef Long's way of trying to make classic Middle Eastern flavors more approachable.

You'll note that the menu lists the origin of many of the ingredients used. That's because Chef Long believes, as many of today's chefs do, that "there needs to be a high level of transparency on menus. If it's from a local farm, then put it on the menu and then only serve that thing. I, as a chef, feel a level of responsibility to showcase the hard work and craftsmanship of local food producers."

SEARED SCALLOPS WITH CHARRED EASTERN SHORE SWEET CORN, AVOCADO PUREE & POTATO CROUTONS

(SERVES 4)

15 ears sweet Eastern Shore corn

2 pounds U-10 scallops, or largest available

4 ripe avocados

Juice of 3 limes

Salt, to taste

8 ounces heavy whipping cream

8 ounces mascarpone cheese

1 teaspoon turmeric

2 large Idaho potatoes

1 tablespoon olive oil (divided)

1 tablespoon cold butter

Chopped parsley, for garnish

Shuck the corn, being careful to remove all of the silk. Cook the corn on a clean, hot grill until soft and slightly charred (dots of black on about half of the kernels). Set aside to cool.

Examine your scallops. If they have a little rectangular tag of tissue on one side, remove and discard it. Place the scallops on a plate lined with several paper towels to remove some of the moisture; this helps achieve a better sear when cooking. Refrigerate until ready to cook.

Dice the avocado and place in a blender with the lime juice. Blend to a puree and add salt to taste. Store in the refrigerator until ready to use. If you have a squeeze bottle, pour the puree into the bottle before refrigerating.

Slice the kernels of corn from the cobs, being careful not to cut into the cob. Place the corn in a medium-size pot and add the cream, mascarpone, and turmeric. Bring the mixture to a simmer over medium heat, taking care not to let it boil. Turn down the heat and continue to simmer for about 20 minutes, or until thick. If preparing the dish immediately, reduce heat to the lowest level possible while preparing the remainder of the dish; otherwise cool and refrigerate.

Cut the potatoes into ¼-inch dice. Heat 2 teaspoons of olive oil in a skillet over medium heat. Add the diced potatoes and toss until evenly coated. Cover and steam until soft, about 3 minutes. When the potatoes soften, remove the lid and toss them in the skillet. Increase the heat to medium-high. Stir every minute or so until the potatoes are light brown and crispy.

When ready to put the dish together, reheat the corn if necessary.

Season the scallops to taste with salt and pepper. Place 1 teaspoon of olive oil in large sauté pan and swirl to coat the bottom. Place on high heat. When wisps of smoke start coming off the edges of the pan, place the scallops in the pan with at least 1 inch of space between them. (Tip: Start at the top of the pan—12:00 position—and work clockwise around the pan). Cook the scallops without touching them for about 2 minutes or until the bottoms are golden brown, then gently turn each scallop. Wait 1 minute more, remove the pan from the heat, and add the butter—a French technique called mounting with butter, which will add a rich buttery finish to the outside of the scallops and gently finish cooking them. Allow the scallops to rest in the pan while plating the corn.

Place two ladles of creamed corn in each of four large bowls. Arrange scallops in a tight pile in the middle. Place a large dot of avocado puree on each scallop—here's where the squeeze bottle really helps. Add a handful of potato croutons. Garnish with chopped parsley.

Grilled Whole Striped Bass
with Crispy Brussels Sprouts, Golden Raisins, Pine Nuts & Pomegranate Molasses

(SERVES 2)

"The fish selected will have a big impact on this dish. When selecting a fish, check for three things: clear eyes, clean smell (not fishy), and the body firm and stiff to the touch. Have the fishmonger scale and gut the fish for you before taking it home."

1 pound brussels sprouts
2 ounces pine nuts
1 (1½-pound) whole striped bass
1 ounce fresh thyme sprigs
1 ounce rosemary
Salt and pepper
Canola oil, for deep-frying
1 tablespoon cold butter
1 tablespoon golden raisins
4 tablespoons pomegranate molasses

Quarter the brussels sprouts lengthwise and set aside.

Toast the pine nuts in a 325°F oven for a few minutes until light brown. Keep at room temperature.

Rinse the fish and pat dry with a paper towel. Stuff the body cavity with the thyme and rosemary. Score the skin of the fish several times on each side. Season with salt and pepper.

Grill the fish over high heat, about 7 minutes on each side. Do not move the fish until it lifts from the grill easily, otherwise the skin may be damaged. To test for doneness, slide a thin metal skewer into the middle of the fish above the body cavity; the fish is fully cooked when the entire skewer comes out hot.

While the fish is cooking on the grill, put 2 inches of canola oil in a medium pot and place on high heat until the oil is hot. (Tip: Place 1 popcorn kernel in the oil. When the kernel pops, the oil is the correct temperature.) Carefully add the brussels sprouts. Reduce the heat to medium-high and fry the sprouts until slightly brown on the edges, about 3 minutes. Remove with a strainer. Place in a mixing bowl and toss with butter, salt and pepper, the raisins, toasted pine nuts, and 2 tablespoons of the pomegranate molasses.

Place the brussels sprouts in the middle of a large platter. Place the whole fish on top of the sprouts. Drizzle with the rest of the pomegranate molasses. Serve family style.

Great Sage

5809 Clarksville Square Drive
Clarksville, MD 21029
(443) 535-9400
greatsage.com
Owners: Jeff Kaufman, Holly Kaufman, Jody Cutler
Chef: Adam Pierce

Conscious Corner is a cluster of shops selling socially responsible and organic goods in the town of Clarksville in Howard County. Bark! is a pet store. Nest sells housewares, clothing, kids' stuff, and accessories, and Boulder sells men's clothing. Roots is a food market that sells only clean food. Then there's Great Sage, a vegan restaurant that joined the Corner in 2004. And a welcome addition it was to an area full of restaurants perfect for omnivores and carnivores but sorely lacking in places where vegetarians and especially vegans could find a wide variety of choices for lunch, dinner, and weekend brunch.

Lest you imagine a patchouli-scented room with hemp curtains and brown rice on every plate, let us assure you that Great Sage boasts a sophisticated and modern decor that is both warm and inviting. It's actually a perfect spot for a romantic night out with your sweetheart . . . or Sunday brunch with Grandma and the kids . . . or lunch with girlfriends. The creative cuisine by Chef Adam Pierce reflects the influences of many cultures, from Mexico to France to Southeast Asia. And yes, every bit of it is free of animal products of any kind.

Chef Pierce started out at Great Sage as the head baker, then worked his way up the line to executive chef, a position he's held for over two years now. While not a vegan himself, he prefers to eat organically and believes in the importance of knowing where one's food comes from. While sticking within a fairly strict set of culinary guidelines might be a challenge for the omnivorous chef, Chef Pierce finds it more of a "fun game to create great dishes for everyone to enjoy." And while Great Sage serves only vegan food, not all of the restaurant's customers adhere to such a strict diet. Ask any of them and they will tell you that they come because Chef Pierce's food is innovative and delicious and can make even the most avowed carnivore forget meat for a little while. The "crab" cakes made with hearts of palm, which mimic the texture of blue crab amazingly well, are among our personal favorites and can be made at home with great success.

HEARTS OF PALM CRAB CAKES WITH CAPER REMOULADE

(SERVES 4)

You'll need a kitchen scale to measure out the vegetables and bread crumbs, as the measurements are by weight; the liquid ingredients like the Veganaise and mustard are by volume, so a measuring cup will do.

For the caper remoulade:

1 ounce diced red onion
1½ ounces capers
1 tablespoon diced sun-dried tomato
⅓ stalk celery, diced
½ cup Veganaise
1 teaspoon lemon juice
2 teaspoons Dijon mustard
1 tablespoon chopped cilantro

For the cakes:

2 (14-ounce) cans hearts of palm, preferably Native Forest brand
1 teaspoon olive oil
½ teaspoon salt
¼ teaspoon ground black pepper
4 ounces diced red onion
2½ ounces diced celery
2½ ounces diced red bell pepper

2¼ ounces diced poblano pepper
1 teaspoon lemon juice
3 ounces Veganaise
1 ounce Dijon mustard
2 teaspoons Old Bay seasoning
3 ounces gluten-free bread crumbs

To make the caper remoulade: Combine the onion, capers, sun-dried tomatoes, and celery in a food processor and pulse until minced.

Add the remaining ingredients and pulse into a mostly smooth but still somewhat chunky sauce.

To make the cakes: Preheat oven to 350°F.

Toss the hearts of palm with the olive oil, salt, and pepper and place on a sheet pan in a single layer. Bake for 25 minutes, rotating halfway through.

Sauté the onion, celery, and peppers in a bit of olive oil over medium heat until the onions are translucent and the peppers aromatic, about 5 minutes.

When the hearts of palm are cool enough to handle, break them up into a mixing bowl, removing and discarding any "woody" pieces. Add the cooked vegetable mixture along with the lemon juice, Veganaise, Dijon mustard, and Old Bay.

Stir in the bread crumbs and form into four patties. Bake the patties at 350°F for 15 minutes, or until heated through.

Serve with caper remoulade.

Raw White Chocolate Raspberry Tart

(SERVES 8–10)

A raw vegan diet consists of unprocessed, raw plant foods that have not been heated above 104°F. Advocates believe that raw foods have natural enzymes that are killed during the cooking process and can leave toxins behind. This tart is 100 percent nontoxic and 200 percent delicious. While the almond and date crust isn't quite like a baked pastry crust, the filling is creamy and delightful and the ganache tasty enough to eat straight from the bowl with a big spoon.

For the crust:

3 cups whole raw almonds
¼ cup coconut oil
2 cups dried dates, pitted

For the filling:

4 cups raw cashews, soaked for at least 2 hours
⅔ cup agave syrup
Pinch of salt
2 teaspoons vanilla extract
1 vanilla bean, scraped
8 ounces cocoa butter (found in most health food stores)
⅔ cup coconut oil
10 ounces fresh or frozen raspberries

For the ganache:

1 cup raw cacao powder
1 cup agave syrup
1 cup coconut oil
Pinch of salt

To make the crust: Process the almonds in a food processor until very fine. Add the coconut oil and dates and pulse until a dough forms. Press this dough into the bottom of a springform pan and chill until the filling is ready.

To make the filling: Using a food processor or high-power blender, combine all filling ingredients except the raspberries. You may need to melt the cocoa butter slightly for it to blend better.

Place the raspberries on the almond crust evenly and pour the cocoa butter–cashew mixture over the berries. Let set in the refrigerator until solid, at least 1 hour.

To make the ganache: Pulse all the ganache ingredients in the food processor until smooth. Taste for saltiness and sweetness and add a few drops more agave or a bit more salt if necessary. Don't add too much more agave, or the ganache will not set properly.

Remove the collar from the springform pan and pour the ganache over the refrigerated tart. Allow the glaze to set until totally firm before cutting into wedges and serving.

GRILLE 620

11099 RESORT ROAD
ELLICOTT CITY, MD 21042
(410) 203-0620
FACEBOOK.COM/GRILLE620
OWNERS: ALI SADEGHI, GABY HADDAD, ADALIUS THOMAS
CHEF: FABIO MURA

After many years in the restaurant business working for companies like Ruth's Chris, Ali Sadeghi and Gaby Haddad decided to put their combined industry knowledge together and open a restaurant of their own. They partnered with longtime friend Adalius Thomas, a former Baltimore Ravens linebacker, to open Grille 620, in the new Turf Valley Town Square development in Ellicott City.

While one might think the restaurant would be decorated in Ravens purple and black, rather it is all creams and browns, with accents of reclaimed wood from barns and a wall made of planks from old bourbon barrels. In the front, the bar area serves a menu of burgers and other sandwiches to go with specialty cocktails, bourbon and tequila that the house extra-ages in custom-made oak barrels, and sixteen rotating taps of craft beers that can include local favorites like Flying Dog and Heavy Seas. We're perfectly happy to munch on a Yum Yum Burger topped with pork belly, a fried egg, cheese, *and* béarnaise, but for more elegant food we head into the dining room. The menu there features steak and seafood and is described by Chef Fabio Mura as "Modern American with a little fusion."

Chef Mura hails from the Italian island of Sardinia, where he learned to cook from his grandmothers, aunts, and mother before heading off to culinary school. "Being Italian you start at an early age. Sunday used to be big family lunch. We would start cooking at seven or eight a.m. to be ready around one p.m. You sit and don't get up for a few hours," Mura says with a chuckle. He spent his early career working in Italy and Sardinia, learning various Italian cuisines. Coming to the United States, Mura worked at Sotto Sopra and Chazz: A Bronx Original before landing at Grille 620.

An Italian influence is evident in some dishes, like a bruschetta topped with pancetta and a white bean mousse, the gnocchi, and the squid ink pasta, but Asia peeks out from others. Togarashi, a peppery Japanese condiment, just seems right on an ahi tuna entree; likewise the honey miso flavoring on a piece of tender salmon. But despite the fusion touches, the dishes at Grille 620 are largely unfussy. "I like crisp, bold flavors," says Chef Mura. "The main ingredient of your dish should speak for itself. Simplicity is key."

GRILLED OCTOPUS
WITH BEAN SALAD & BABY ARUGULA
(SERVES 4)

For the octopus:

2 tablespoons extra virgin olive oil
4 garlic cloves, thinly sliced
1 teaspoon hot red pepper flakes
1 (2-pound) octopus, fresh or frozen
1 lemon, cut in half

For the vinaigrette:

Juice of 1 lemon
1 tablespoon chopped capers
1½ teaspoons hot red pepper flakes
½ cup extra virgin olive oil
Kosher salt, to taste
Black pepper, finely ground, to taste

For the beans:

1 cup cannellini beans, cooked
1 tablespoon red wine vinegar
3 tablespoons extra virgin olive oil
½ red onion, finely chopped
1 tablespoon chopped fresh parsley

For serving:

1 cup baby arugula

To make the octopus: Preheat an oven to 300°F.

In a large dutch oven, heat the olive oil over high heat until almost smoking. Add the garlic and red pepper flakes and cook for 2 minutes. Add the octopus to the pan and, still over high heat, cook on all sides until it has changed color and has released its liquid. Add the lemon, cover the pan with aluminum foil instead of its lid, and bake for 1½–1¾ hours, or until the octopus is soft. Cool to room temperature.

Carefully separate the octopus tentacles from the head. Cut the tentacles into 4-inch pieces; cut the head in half.

To make the vinaigrette: Bring the lemon juice and capers to a boil in a small saucepan and reduce by half, to a syrupy consistency. Add the red pepper flakes and let cool. Once cool, whisk in the olive oil. Add salt and pepper to taste.

To make the beans: Toss the beans with the red wine vinegar, extra virgin olive oil, chopped onion, and parsley, and allow the mixture to marinate before serving, about 1 hour.

Preheat grill to very high. Grill the octopus pieces until both sides have grill marks. Slice them into 1–2 inches and tossed with lemon-caper vinaigrette.

To serve: Place bean salad in the center of each plate, topped with grilled octopus and baby arugula.

GRILLED SHRIMP WITH MANGO CHUTNEY

(SERVES 2)

For the vinaigrette:

Juice of 1 lemon
½ cup extra virgin olive oil
1 tablespoon chopped Italian parsley
Salt and black pepper, to taste

For the mango chutney:

1 ripe mango, peeled and diced
1 jalapeño, seeded and diced
Juice of 1 lime
¼ cup diced red pepper
1 tablespoon honey
1 tablespoon chopped cilantro
Salt, to taste

For the shrimp:

12 (21–25 count) shrimp
12 spears asparagus, trimmed

To make the vinaigrette: Whisk together the lemon juice and olive oil. Stir in the parsley and season with salt and pepper to taste.

To make the chutney: Combine all ingredients in a bowl. Let rest for 2–3 hours to allow flavors to develop.

To make the shrimp and asparagus: Peel and devein the shrimp, leaving the tails on. Place the shrimp in a bowl and pour half the vinaigrette over. Place the asparagus in a separate bowl and coat with the remaining vinaigrette. Refrigerate both shrimp and asparagus for no longer than 30 minutes.

Heat a charcoal or gas grill to high, or heat a grill pan over high heat. Add the asparagus, cooking 5–10 minutes, depending on the thickness of the spears, until tender. Cook the shrimp until opaque, about 2 minutes per side.

To serve: Arrange the asparagus on a platter. Top with the shrimp. Spoon over the mango chutney, making sure to also spoon over the liquid at the bottom of the chutney bowl.

Iron Bridge Wine Company

10435 Maryland 108
Columbia, MD 21044
(410) 997-3456
IRONBRIDGEWINES.COM
OWNERS: ROB WECKER, STEVE WECKER
CHEF: CHRIS LEWIS

When Rob ("Wine Geek") and Steve ("Idea Guy") Wecker opened Iron Bridge Wine Company more than a decade ago, they sought to fill the needs of restaurant patrons who wanted a great glass of wine with dinner but didn't want to have to pay for a full bottle to get it. So Iron Bridge offers thirty or so wines from small vineyards all over the world, sold by the glass every day. And if someone is in the mood for multiple glasses, or wants to take some home, Iron Bridge sells wine in bottles too, with more than three hundred wines in stock at about one-third of restaurant prices. There's a small corkage fee if they're sampled in-house.

Of course, all of that fancy grape juice needs some good food to accompany it, and that's where Chef Chris Lewis steps in. Chef Lewis, who graduated from the Pennsylvania School of Culinary Arts, has been at Iron Bridge Wine Company since 2011. The Carroll County native worked as sous-chef for both the Milton Inn and Linwood's and was executive chef at an old Baltimore favorite, the dear departed Brass Elephant. In 2012 and 2013 he came in second in the Mason Dixon Master Chef Tournament, but at Iron Bridge, Lewis is number one in the kitchen.

His menu at Iron Bridge Wine Company is ever changing, which Chef Lewis considers fun. When asked how he comes up with dishes that are meant to be eaten as an accompaniment to a nice glass of wine (or the other way around if, like us, you're more of a food person than a wine person!), he says, "We always create the dish first, then taste it. Then

we think about the wine aspect. Is it too sweet? Salty? Sour? If so, we find the balance and create it again."

Chef Lewis's seasonal menu runs the gamut from obvious wine-friendly nibbles like cheese and charcuterie plates that include house-made pâté and brawn (aka head cheese) to something more delicate, like a gazpacho with spiced shrimp. There are also hearty entrees such as lamb ravioli with lamb bacon, and a burger made with local Roseda Farms beef. Much of the product Chef Lewis uses comes from local farms like Discovery Farms and Rebecca's Garden, both nearby in Howard County. "Buying locally ensures we have the freshest ingredients," he says.

"I became a chef for my love of food and respect for animals. It is such a rush to have a busy service and then have so many people leave your establishment knowing that they had a great time."

Pecan Tart

(MAKES ONE 12-INCH TART)

For the crust:

2½ cups flour
1½ tablespoons sugar
½ pound unsalted butter, cubed
6 tablespoons ice water

For the filling:

¾ cup unsalted butter
¾ cup sugar
¾ cup light brown sugar
1½ cups corn syrup
1 teaspoon kosher salt
4½ teaspoons bourbon
1½ teaspoons vanilla extract
6 eggs, beaten
1½ cups whole pecans

To make the crust: Stir together the flour and sugar. Place in the bowl of a stand mixer and add the butter. Mix on medium-low speed until the texture resembles coarse cornmeal. Add the water slowly and mix on low speed just until the dough comes together.

Transfer the dough to a work surface. Pat into a ball and flatten into a disk. Wrap in plastic and refrigerate.

To make the filling: In a saucepan, combine butter, sugars, corn syrup, salt, bourbon, and vanilla. Bring the mixture to a boil, then remove from heat. Allow to cool for about 5 minutes before whisking in the eggs.

To assemble and bake the pie: Preheat oven to 350°F.

Remove the chilled pie dough and roll out into a 15-inch-diameter circle about ¼ inch thick. Place in a 12-inch tart pan with a removable bottom. Decoratively crimp edges above the top lip of the pan. If you happen to make any holes in the crust during this process, patch with leftover dough.

Spread the pecans in the shell, and pour in batter to just below the rim.

Place the pie on a cookie sheet to catch drips and bake for 20 minutes, until the edges are set and the center is still slightly loose. If the crust seems to be browning excessively, cover it with aluminum foil partway through the baking.

Allow to cool completely before serving.

Laurrapin Grille

209 N Washington Street
Havre de Grace, MD 21078
(410) 939-4956
LAURRAPIN.COM
OWNERS: CHEF BRUCE CLARKE, SHERIFA CLARKE

When Bruce Clarke was twelve years old, he decided he had had enough of his mother's traditional home-style cooking. His father challenged him to do better. Bruce took the challenge, and by the time he was eighteen, his parents didn't want him to leave home, lest they miss out on his boeuf bourguignonne or coq au vin. But the cooking bug had bitten him hard, and Bruce left to make a name for himself as a chef.

Chef Clarke trained at the Harbor Court Hotel and eventually worked at several of the area's finest restaurants. Years later, when he was the chef-owner of Timber Creek in Kingsville, he met his future wife, Sherifa. The two found that they shared a love for

food, but also for kayaking, particularly in the small community of Havre de Grace. It seemed like the perfect place to open a restaurant that would celebrate the bounty of meats and produce from local farms and the seafood of the nearby Chesapeake Bay.

The name of the restaurant comes from the southern term for full-of-flavor "po' folks food." This is reflected in the menu with down-home favorites like mac and cheese and Eastern Shore Fried Chicken, but there's also a bit of international flair with items like the always in-demand Argentinian Pot Roast and the equally popular Thai pork burger.

Laurrapin sources as much product as possible from local farms, and the menu tells you exactly where everything comes from. "Most of the dishes served at Laurrapin are prepared with local ingredients," says Chef Bruce. "Our menu changes frequently because we buy whole animals 'by the hoof,' so we work our way through all the different cuts."

Bruce and Sherifa Clarke are so committed to using local ingredients that they've even started their own garden on land provided by Mt. Felix Farm, a local vineyard and winery whose wine they feature. They've also incorporated environmentally responsible practices like composting and reclaiming water into their business.

VEGGIE WELLINGTON

(SERVES 4)

For the filling:

1 small zucchini, cut in small dice
1 small yellow squash, cut in small dice
1 small red pepper, cut in small dice
1 teaspoon minced garlic
¼ cup olive oil
½ cup balsamic vinaigrette
4–6 basil leaves, sliced thinly in a chiffonade
4 medium-to-large portobello mushrooms
Salt and pepper, to taste

For the Wellington:

1 sheet frozen puff pastry
12 ounces heavy cream
2 ounces sun-dried tomato paste
1 bunch asparagus, trimmed
Olive oil
Salt and pepper, to taste

To make the filling: Toss the squashes, pepper, and garlic with the olive oil and balsamic vinaigrette. Refrigerate for at least 2 hours or overnight.

Preheat oven to 350°F.

Remove the stems from the mushrooms and scoop out the gills with a spoon. Brush both sides of the mushroom caps with a little olive oil, place them on a baking sheet, and roast for about 10 minutes per side.

Remove the vegetables from the marinade, season with salt and pepper, and spread on a separate baking sheet. Roast for 5–7 minutes.

To make the Wellington: Preheat oven to 350°F.

Thaw the pastry and unroll into a flat sheet. Cut into four equal squares. Place a roasted mushroom at the center of each pastry square, cup side up. Divide the filling evenly between the mushrooms. Fold the pastry corners up over the stuffing and invert the mushroom packets onto a greased baking sheet. Bake until golden brown, about 15–20 minutes.

While the Wellingtons are baking, bring the cream to a boil in a large saucepan. Add the sun-dried tomato paste, turn the heat to medium, and reduce the liquid by half, about 10 minutes. Stir frequently, and watch carefully so the cream does not scorch on the bottom of the pan.

In a baking pan, toss the asparagus with a little olive oil and salt and pepper. Roast until tender; time will vary depending on thickness of asparagus.

To plate: Arrange equal amounts of asparagus on four plates. Divide the sauce evenly over the asparagus and place the wellingtons on top.

Shrimp & Grits

(SERVES 4)

For the grits:

1 ounce olive oil

4 ounces tasso ham, cut in small dice

2⅔ cups whole milk

2 cups white grits

¼ cup heavy cream

4 ounces white cheddar, grated

Salt and pepper, to taste

For the shrimp:

16 large Gulf Coast shrimp, peeled and deveined

1 ounce olive oil

1–2 ounces blackening spice

1 teaspoon minced garlic

Juice of ½ lemon

4 ounces dry white wine

6 tablespoons cold unsalted butter

1 scallion, cut on the bias into thin slices

To make the grits: Heat the oil in a heavy-bottomed pot and add the tasso. Reduce heat and render the ham for 2–3 minutes. Add the milk; turn up heat, and bring to a boil.

Stir in the grits and simmer for 10 minutes, until tender, adding additional milk if needed.

Stir in the cheese, allowing it to melt into the grits. Remove from heat, add the cream, and season with salt and pepper. Keep warm.

To make the shrimp: Coat the shrimp on both sides with olive oil and sprinkle with blackening spice, using more or less to taste.

Heat a heavy-bottomed sauté pan. Turn the exhaust fan to high or open a window. Add the shrimp to pan and cook for 2 minutes on one side, then turn and cook for 1 minute more.

Add the garlic to the pan and stir for 30 seconds. Remove the shrimp and set aside. Add the lemon juice and wine, bring to a boil, and reduce by half.

Stir in the butter. Remove the pan from the heat, making sure the butter melts completely.

To serve: Scoop grits onto four plates. Arrange the shrimp over the grits. Spoon the sauce over the shrimp and garnish with sliced scallion.

The Farms in Farm-to-Table

Marvesta Shrimp

Much of the shrimp sold today is farm raised. Indoor farms, even. Marvesta Shrimp (marvesta.com) can produce the same amount of shrimp in its 5 acres of indoor tanks as other farms using 450 acres of outdoor ponds. Using indoor tanks is beneficial to the environment because there is no discharge into the coastal waters, and it's beneficial to the shrimp since they are protected from airborne viruses. The shrimp are raised in an enclosed ecosystem of Mid-Atlantic ocean water without exposure to antibiotics, hormones, or preservatives. When the shrimp are harvested, instead of the common practice of flash freezing, Marvesta shrimp are put on ice and shipped to area restaurants within 24 hours.

Vin 909

909 Bay Ridge Avenue
Annapolis, MD 21403
(410) 990-1846
vin909.com
Owner: Alex Manfredonia
Chef: Justin Moore

In the Annapolis neighborhood of Eastport sits an inviting red-and-tan Sears Roebuck house surrounded by lush foliage and trees. It's the kind of place where you would want to relax on the patio or snuggle by the fireplace on a cold winter's night, which is exactly the way owner Alex Manfredonia and Executive Chef Justin Moore want it. Vin 909 provides a casual environment for diners to drink wine and enjoy their Mediterranean-influenced dishes.

After working at Bix in San Francisco, Alex and Justin moved east to start their own place that focuses on fresh ingredients and environmentally sound practices. These are terms that are thrown about quite a bit, but Alex and Justin truly live this philosophy, recycling three-quarters of their trash and sourcing a large part of their produce and meats from Groundworks Farm, with whom they have an exclusive arrangement. They even offer a CSA pickup once a week in their parking lot and sell restaurant condiments to pair with the produce. "Using the best ingredients makes the best food," states Chef Moore emphatically. "The best ingredients are things raised with care, not fed antibiotics, happy and free-range and, most of all, at the peak of their season. Knowing your farmer is important, having that trust in what they're producing."

Of course, to bring the customers in, the food has to be good, and it is. From their brick oven, Chef Moore produces what they like to call Eastport Style Pizza: hand-shaped pizzas with a crispy crust. The Spotted Pig, topped with wild boar and sopressata, is one of the most popular. Vin 909 also offers sandos (brick oven sandwiches), soups, salads, and plenty of entrees, but the restaurant has a clear focus on wines. The list features many smaller growers not commonly known and groups them into four basic price ranges to suit all pocketbooks. This unpretentious approach, along with the bright airy environment inside, makes diners feel welcome.

Fried Squash Blossoms
with White Corn Coulis & Black Truffle

(SERVES 2)

12 ears white corn
2 cups diced onion
½ cup chopped celery
4 tablespoons unsalted butter
4 garlic cloves, chopped
1½ cups heavy cream
⅛ cup sugar
Salt, to taste
1 cup all-purpose flour
½ teaspoon piment d'Espelette or paprika
   or black pepper
1½ cups pilsner-style beer
2 quarts vegetable oil for frying
8 large, fresh squash blossoms
½ black truffle (optional)

Shuck the ears of corn and cut off the kernels. Reserve the cobs.

In a large pot, sauté the corn kernels, onion, and celery in the butter for about 5 minutes. Add the garlic and cook for an additional 45 seconds. Add 2½ quarts of water and the reserved corncobs and lightly simmer the mixture for about 20 minutes. Remove the cobs and add the cream and sugar. Simmer for a few minutes more until the sugar is completely dissolved. Remove from heat.

When the corn mixture is cool, puree it in a blender in batches until very smooth. Strain if desired to remove pulp. Add salt to taste.

Make a batter by whisking together the flour and piment d'Espelette with the beer. Season with salt.

In a deep fryer or large heavy pot, heat the vegetable oil to 350°F.

Dip the squash blossoms in the batter, making sure each one is completely coated, and fry them a couple at a time for about 2 minutes, until golden brown. Don't crowd the fryer or they will stick together. When browned, remove the squash blossoms to paper-towel-lined plates and season them with a pinch of salt.

While the squash blossoms are cooking, warm the corn coulis in a small pot.

To serve, ladle some of the coulis onto two plates. Arrange four squash blossoms on each plate. Grate some truffle on top of squash blossoms.

Index

About the Authors

Kathy Wielech Patterson and Neal Patterson are the award-winning writers of the food blog, Minxeats. Their writing has appeared in *Discover Baltimore, Towson Life, Sniffapalooza Magazine,* and other publications. They are also the authors of *Food Lovers' Guide to Baltimore,* published by Globe Pequot in 2013. Neal's work has appeared in the anthologies *The Dead Walk!* and *Hey Kids, Comics!,* and on the website Channel 37: Serial Science Fiction from the Distant Reaches of UHF.

Kathy and Neal live in Baltimore.

Acknowledgments

This project was a somewhat more stressful undertaking than our last book, and we lost a little sleep worrying (and even dreaming) about reformatting recipes! It all came together in the end, however, and we're thankful to several people. First, we'd like to thank our editor, Tracee Williams, who—as our last editor at Globe Pequot, Kevin Sirois, put it—made writing this book a "win-win situation." We appreciate all of her support during this project. And we'd also like to thank our talented photographer, Kevin Maher. He put many miles on his car driving from his home on the Eastern Shore to Baltimore in order to beautify our words with his images.

We'd like also to thank all of the chefs, restaurant employees, and PR folks who generously donated their recipes, time, and information, and for being there for last-minute phone calls, answering tons of e-mails asking questions (and more e-mails asking even more questions), and arranging their schedules to accommodate us and Kevin. Special thanks to Dara Bunjon, Kit Waskom Pollard, Jamie Watt Arnold, Amy Burke Friedman, and Marianne Ortiz for their continued support and for being generally amazing.